GASLIGHTING

GASLIGHTING

A Step-by-Step Recovery Guide
to Heal from Emotional Abuse
and Build Healthy Relationships

Deborah Vinall, PsyD, LMFT

ROCKRIDGE
PRESS

For general information on our other products and services or to obtain technical support, please contact our Customer Care Department within the United States at (866) 744-2665, or outside the United States at (510) 253-0500.

Rockridge Press publishes its books in a variety of electronic and print formats. Some content that appears in print may not be available in electronic books, and vice versa.

Interior and Cover Designer: Francesca Pacchini
Art Producer: Meg Baggott
Editor: Jesse Aylen
Production Editor: Nora Milman
Production Manager: Jose Olivera

Cover illustration ©2021 Collaborate Agency

Author photo courtesy of Weezer Scarborough

ISBN: Print 978-1-64876-649-7 | eBook 978-1-64876-149-2

R1

To Shane:
My partner,
my anchor,
my best friend,
and my love.

CONTENTS

INTRODUCTION AND
HOW TO USE THIS BOOK

Dear reader, I'm so glad you picked up this book. At the same time, I'm also a little bit sorry, because it suggests that you are in a relationship that is not fully satisfying, one in which you may be feeling a bewildering mix of love and attachment interwoven with confusion, hurt, and doubt. Perhaps you feel manipulated, angry, and ashamed, yet unable to identify what is wrong. But I also feel hope and optimism, because your courage in deciding to read this book may be a significant step in changing your life and your relationships for the better.

My name is Deborah Vinall, and I am a doctor of psychology and a licensed marriage and family therapist. Since 2004, I have been working professionally with individuals and couples to improve their relationships and heal from the deep scars left by unhealthy dynamics, whether with parents, relatives, romantic partners, or other encounters and experiences. With a specialty in trauma, I help people overcome a myriad of acute and chronic traumatic experiences. In my practice, I've seen firsthand that for some, emotional abuse may leave the deepest scars.

Gaslighting is one particularly insidious form of emotional abuse. Gaslighting can be a primary pattern of behavior, or more commonly, it can serve to cover up for and deflect responsibility away from emotional or other types of abuse. It can be an entrenched pattern or an occasional but unhealthy response. Gaslighting may happen in an intimate relationship, like a domestic partnership or parent-child dynamic, a friendship, an institution such as a church, workplace, or school, or larger societal and political constructs. No matter where it happens, gaslighting leads you to doubt yourself and question your reality.

Know that you have the power to identify these dynamics, break free from them, and heal from their corrosive effects. Using proven techniques and demonstrative fictional narratives, this book will help empower you with knowledge, confidence, and practical steps to reclaiming your sense of self in relationships and in the world.

The goal is not to change the gaslighter, because unless they desire inner growth, such change can be no more than a fantasy. But when you change yourself, you change the dynamic, whether you choose to remain in the relationship or not. You can heal from what you have endured, find clarity, and develop healthier relationships in the present and future.

As you move through this book, take time to pause and reflect. I gently encourage you to read it in order so that your understanding builds from the initial chapters' conceptual foundation to the skills laid out in the seven steps in part 2. Work through the simple exercises, noting the feedback produced in the process and your internal reactions. If you find yourself feeling highly activated or flooded by memories, be kind to yourself: Pause, take a break, breathe deeply, reset. There is always time to continue growth and healing. When you are ready, take a breath, and let's begin.

PART ONE GASLIGHTING AND EMOTIONAL ABUSE

The first step to healing and change is identifying what is happening in your life. This section will discuss what gaslighting is, the common tactics gaslighters use, and the impacts of this and other forms of emotional abuse. In part 2, we will walk through seven steps to breaking the chains of gaslighting, healing, and establishing healthy relationships in your life. Take your time as you work through these chapters. Allow yourself curiosity, grief, and anger, but most of all, hope. Change is ahead.

1

CHAPTER 1:
UNDERSTANDING GASLIGHTING

Gaslighting is a form of manipulation, deception, and control that makes you doubt your own perceptions and memories. We will take a closer look at these concepts in the pages ahead, exploring the ways gaslighters maneuver to curate the picture of the world most advantageous to their objectives and designs. We will also look at common characteristics of gaslighters and provide tools to help you assess whether you might be experiencing gaslighting.

WHAT IS GASLIGHTING?

The scene opens in grainy shades of gray. Bella demurely confronts her husband, Paul, and expresses her feelings of shame at watching him flirt with the maid right in front of her. Paul flatly denies what we have witnessed, coldly reprimanding, "You know perfectly well how you imagine things, my dear."

This exchange from the 1940 film *Gaslight* illustrates the then-unlabeled form of emotional abuse that came to be named for the movie. In the film, Paul takes calculated aim at his wife's sanity by coldly denying what she has seen and heard. He falsely accuses her of acts she has no recollection of committing, with the goal of having her committed to an asylum and availing himself of the fortune hidden within the home. When Paul prowls about upstairs in search of hidden

3

gems, Bella observes gaslights dimming, evidence that lights from the shared fuel source are being lit elsewhere. Nevertheless, Paul and the housemaid insist that he was not at home and she must be imagining things. The term gaslighting has come to represent such "crazy-making" lies and behaviors.

Gaslighters follow standard patterns of psychological control. They deny what you have clearly observed, make unfounded accusations, and punish you for supposed infractions. They control the narrative about your sanity to those around you. Such actions alienate the person being gaslit from potential allies who might help them recognize the pattern and stand firm, set boundaries, or escape. This also creates a secondary gaslighting target, as these witnesses may be manipulated, too, discarding their own observations in favor of the explanation provided by the authoritative, ostensibly self-controlled, and often charismatic gaslighter.

Gaslighters frequently accuse you of being "too emotional," "crazy," "hysterical," "forgetful," or an outright liar. Such accusations serve to deflect attention from the gaslighter. These labels provide an explanation for the discrepancy between what you experience and the story they tell. They eliminate grounds for argument, because any retort can be absorbed by the framework of hysteria or insanity constructed by the gaslighter. You may find yourself having to choose between allegiance to someone who is important to you and your own intuitive or sensory knowledge.

Although "gaslighter" is not a diagnostic term, it has colloquially come to represent a person who consistently displays this pattern of behavior. Gaslighters often exhibit symptoms of personality disorders or enduring patterns of maladaptive behavior, such as narcissism or sociopathy. As with any behavior, there are needs and motivations driving these patterns. We will explore these later when we break down the various types of gaslighters. For now, it may suffice to recognize the irony that the very people throwing out labels of "crazy" are frequently harboring a significant degree of mental pathology themselves.

Nevertheless, perhaps they do make you feel a little "crazy," and this makes it hard to determine whether what you're dealing with really is gaslighting. To help answer this crucial question, take a look at the following quiz.

IS IT GASLIGHTING?

Is what you are experiencing really gaslighting? The catch-22 of answering these questions is that by nature, gaslighting causes you to doubt yourself and your intuition. Sometimes an objective assessment tool can help sort through that conflict. Try to answer these questions as honestly as you can, trusting your gut instinct.

Check those that apply:

☐ Do you often question yourself, wondering whether your memory is accurate?

☐ Do you feel that you can't trust your emotions?

☐ Do you often fear that others won't believe the truthful things you say?

☐ Do you find your recalled version of events frequently challenged?

☐ Do you feel as though most or all conflicts are your fault?

☐ Does talking to that certain someone leave you feeling "a little crazy"?

☐ Do they often suggest or insinuate that you are "too emotional"?

☐ Do you feel less than or smaller when talking with them and unsure why?

☐ Do they emphasize their presumed position of authority?

☐ Do they diminish, laugh at, ignore, or devalue your feelings and experiences?

☐ Do they consistently downplay your accomplishments, while celebrating their own?

☐ Do they never seem to admit fault?

☐ Do you leave encounters with them questioning what is wrong with you?

☐ Do you find yourself questioning whether it really is as bad as it seems?

If you answered yes to more than ten of these questions, you likely have a toxic relationship with an emotionally abusive gaslighter.

If you scored between eight and ten, chances are high that you are in an unhealthy relationship that involves a significant amount of gaslighting.

If you resonated with six to eight of these descriptors, you may have someone in your life who gaslights you at times.

Even if you scored lower than six but connected strongly with some descriptors, this book may be of help to you. Perhaps you've lived with gaslighting or other emotional abuse in the past. The steps to freedom will help you gain confidence and establish healthier relationships.

As you took this quiz, did you feel validated in seeing your lived experience described? Perhaps you felt a sinking sense of anxiety, revulsion, or horror. Maybe you feel a dawning hope, knowing that in recognizing the problem, change can begin. Whatever came up for you, just notice that. Your feelings, no matter what they are, are valid. Your emotions and perceptions matter, and you can trust them.

RECOGNIZING GASLIGHTING BEHAVIOR

Vanya had trouble trusting her partner. She came to therapy after he repeatedly made angry suggestions that she needed to work on her "trust issues." He constantly accused her of flirting with other men, and she started to question her own intentions even when chatting with colleagues. When his accusations extended to comments about her "flirting problem" to their mutual friends, she withdrew in embarrassment, leading to fewer social gatherings.

At home, she tried not to react when she saw him tilt his phone away during lengthy text exchanges and didn't argue when he explained that the condoms in the glove box were "just in case" they decided to go camping together. When she found fewer condoms the next time, he laughed and said she was imagining things. Vanya started to wonder whether perhaps he was right.

They had good times, and their sexual chemistry was strong. So why did something feel off? The problem must be her, she concluded. He wasn't wrong in pointing out her mental illness— she had been feeling depressed and anxious. Maybe she really was "crazy."

The first step in breaking free from the bonds of gaslighting is naming the problem. To borrow a signature phrase from psychiatrist Daniel Siegel, "You've got to name it to tame it." When we find language to describe experiences that evoke strong emotions, we shift from primary activation of the reactive-emotional brain to our analytical-logical brain region, where we are better able to solve problems. When you name gaslighting for what it is, you take the first step in reclaiming a sense of control in a situation that was crafted to leave you feeling out of control.

From what we've discussed, perhaps you can see how Vanya was being gaslit. Maybe it's becoming clearer how being able to name the problem is key to finding freedom. It can be much more difficult to identify gaslighting from the inside.

You may have grown up with a gaslighting parent, with such patterns persisting as far back as you can remember. You may have a friendship that leaves you frustrated and frequently questioning yourself or a boss who repeatedly suggests you've made mistakes that you are sure you haven't. Maybe you've been part of a religious community where the need to project an image of purity to outsiders leads to a pattern of "little white lies" or outright denials of what you have witnessed. Or perhaps you live in a country or region led by politicians or other public figures who so frequently deny reality that it is hard to differentiate between what you thought you knew and what you are told. All such experiences can leave you feeling off-balance, and all these scenarios may reflect gaslighting. There is no single, common framework in which gaslighting may occur.

With gaslighting taking so many forms, how can you know whether it's happening to you? Consider what you have learned thus far, weigh the quiz results, and stop and listen within. What is your intuition whispering (or shouting)? What do your felt senses tell you? Take a moment to scan your body. Do you have tension or tightness anywhere? Perhaps you feel a knot in your belly or notice your breath becoming shallow. Are your shoulders tensing, hunching upward, or drawing forward? Does your throat feel constricted, or is there tension in your forehead, around your eyes, or around your mouth? Are your arms or legs tensed?

Close your eyes and notice what you feel. Wherever you find tension, pause and let your attention rest there. Just notice what comes up as you focus your attention inward. Allow your felt sense, your most primitive wisdom, to guide you to your intuitive knowledge, and trust that intuition.

If you suspect you are being gaslit, you probably are.

THE ROLE OF PERSONALITY DISORDERS

In my practice I have worked with many survivors of human trafficking. These individuals were typically coerced by traffickers who took the roles of boyfriend, protector, and ultimately, exploiter. Traffickers use a combination of strategies that include compliments, attentiveness, gifts, rage, shaming, insults, dehumanization, self-pity, demands, violence, gaslighting, and manipulation to extort others to "work" for them.

Traffickers exemplify antisocial personality disorder (APD), characterized by a depraved indifference to the well-being of others. Such people lie chronically, con others, and lack regard for the law. Individuals with APD, along with other cluster B personality disorders such as narcissistic personality disorder (NPD), histrionic personality disorder (HPD), and borderline personality disorder (BPD), frequently employ gaslighting tactics as standard ways of interacting with others. Each type uses gaslighting to manipulate and control others to satisfy desires for power, significance, excitement, or affection. The frequency and intentionality in employing such tactics varies, with APD the most calculating and BPD the most reactive.

Personality disorders reflect deeply ingrained, pervasive patterns of behavior that are not readily amenable to change. They stem from years of childhood neglect, abuse, or maltreatment that was never adaptively faced and resolved. While we can have empathy for the hurt soul inside, the fantasy of fixing the cluster B personality disordered person by enduring the abuse and loving them through it is generally just that—fantasy. No one will change if they don't recognize the need for change and actively pursue it. The only appropriate response is to set firm boundaries that will protect yourself, whether in or out of relationship with them.

SOMEONE DOESN'T NEED TO HAVE A PERSONALITY DISORDER TO BE MANIPULATIVE

Although it can be helpful to have a frame of reference, it is important to remember that you (or even your therapist, unless they've met) cannot diagnose this person. While there is a significant overlap between gaslighting and cluster B personality disorders, unfortunately many people are simply manipulative! For the purposes of your own healing, it is not essential to diagnose them; what is important is to recognize that their behavior is not normal.

Because gaslighting can stem from a variety of pathologies or no diagnosable disorder at all, gaslighters may present very differently. Most are skilled at seeming charming, letting only you see their darker side. This is itself a part of the gaslighting, as you may find yourself wondering why you are the only one who seems to struggle with them. This may lead you to falsely conclude that you are the one with the problem. As you notice certain traits and patterns consistent with personality pathology, allow that awareness to free you of self-blame. You are not at fault. Your responsibility is only to protect yourself and to begin to heal.

Anyone can gaslight, and anyone can be gaslit. Gaslighting may happen in same-gendered relationships, parent-child dynamics, work environments, religious communities, and even political leadership dynamics. The only consistent dynamic is the role of power and control, because establishing and maintaining these things are the gaslighter's primary aims.

More traditional societal gender constructs can influence how gaslighting is used. Historically, men have been socialized to expect authority and deference, and their emotions may be downplayed and dismissed throughout childhood. Combined with common beliefs that men ought to be powerful and dominant, these patterns can set the stage for such individuals to seek power and control through gaslighting. Conversely, women have traditionally been taught to find value in relationships and sexuality. Women are socially conditioned not to communicate their needs assertively, and manipulative tactics too often fill that void. Gaslighting behaviors may be one harmful outcome.

Gaslighting flourishes in people and environments that embrace hierarchical norms. In her research published in the *American Sociological Review* Paige Sweet asserts that gaslighting is fundamentally rooted in social inequalities like gender constructs and serves to reinforce such power structures. Gaslighting may be used to distract from people's experiences of oppression by defending those in positions of dominance. For example, if Tyrone confronts Paul about his racist joke, Paul may wave it off as *"just a joke—don't be so sensitive! Everyone knows I was just kidding."* Worse, Paul may dismiss Tyrone's discomfort, flatly denying that he said anything racist—or that racism even exists. Gaslighting centers the experience of the privileged at the expense of the marginalized party in an unequal society or dynamic.

Likewise, parents may deny children's experience: *"I never said that." "I would never do that." "We're a happy family."* Codependent family members and friends may side with parents to maintain the image of a happy family by minimizing problems seen publicly or by blaming the victim: *"Antonio needs to learn to manage his emotions. If he didn't have so many tantrums, he wouldn't need so many spankings."*

Many transgender individuals experience gaslighting while growing up from those who dismiss their self-knowledge as "just a phase," a sign of mental illness, or rebellious behavior. Even those who have successfully transitioned face gaslighting when people around them refuse or repeatedly "forget" to use their preferred pronouns. Likewise, gay and lesbian youth often battle with gaslighting when those around them suggest they will soon "grow out of it" and can simply choose to embrace a heteronormative life.

Recognizing the gender and other power structures at play beneath the surface of gaslighting is critical to recognizing these patterns as they occur in your life. What you recognize, you gain a measure of control over, and you become empowered to choose your response.

DIFFERENT TYPES OF GASLIGHTERS

It is important to recognize that not all gaslighters are the same. Don't make the mistake of dismissing your experience because it differs from some of the examples. Gaslighting is at its essence simply manipulation and can be used by various types of people for different purposes.

SADISTIC GASLIGHTERS

It is easiest to identify sadistic gaslighters, particularly when you are not in this type of relationship. Sadistic gaslighters intentionally inflict cruelty and consciously take aim at your sense of self. They find dark pleasure in making you doubt yourself and wield this power as a form of control. Sadistic gaslighters may employ gaslighting with flagrant disregard for the psychological consequences, just to entertain an audience or demonstrate power.

However disturbing such antipathy toward the feelings and rights of others may be, less than 4 percent of people show this level of sociopathy. At the same time, a study published in the journal *Partner Abuse* reveals that up to 80 percent of all people experience emotional abuse at some point in their lives, which often involves gaslighting. Clearly, it is not only sociopaths who gaslight.

NARCISSISTIC GASLIGHTERS

Narcissistic gaslighters are consumed with an obsessive focus on themselves. In their unexamined view, others exist to adore or exalt them. They conceal the raw, vulnerable truth of their fear of insignificance and expend enormous energy to cultivate a public perception of greatness. Lacking confidence, they are prone to lash out at those who injure their fragile ego.

Because their self-esteem is so precarious, they must alter the narrative rather than admit fault in any encounter. They cannot be wrong, cruel, or unfair; rather, you are the one who must have misperceived what happened or are somehow at fault. Perhaps what you remembered did not happen at all. Once others accept these distortions, their fear of being exposed as fallible wanes.

DEFENSIVE-INSECURE GASLIGHTERS

Defensive-insecure gaslighters use gaslighting to get out of trouble or avoid the consequences of their actions. They may be parents who have lashed out at their children in ways that they regret but are unable to face or a friend who denies gossiping when confronted by a peer. Their insecurity compels them to hide rather than courageously face the vulnerability of mistakes. They may fear anger, condemnation, or rejection from others if they own messy truths. Rather than embrace imperfection, they desperately gaslight to create an acceptable reality and keep their self-perception intact.

ACCIDENTAL GASLIGHTERS

You may experience gaslighting in a relationship with someone who has undiagnosed memory problems. Such accidental gaslighters are not malicious, though the experience of constantly doubting your reality and memories can be similarly confusing

and disorienting. Accidental gaslighters may have memory diffi-
culties due to poor listening skills, inadequate sleep, an over-busy
schedule, or the effects of a mental illness, a brain lesion, or
dementia. When accidental gaslighters are aware of or can
admit the possibility of their memory deficits, the burden on the
relationship is lighter. When combined with defensiveness or narcissism that interferes with admitting mistakes, memory deficits
can result in problematic dynamics.

YOU CAN HEAL

No matter the dynamic within which gaslighting occurs, the
personality pathology that supports it, or how long you've been
oppressed by it, healing is possible. The paths toward healing and
freedom are similar, no matter the differing patterns and contexts.
You may have felt your power being stripped away, but by picking
up this book and courageously considering these questions, you
have already begun to loosen the chains. You are regaining your
power and, in turn, becoming free.

CHAPTER 2:
THE GASLIGHTER'S PLAYBOOK

In this chapter, we'll examine typical gaslighter patterns and behaviors. As you read, it may be helpful to keep a journal nearby to record any insights, reactions, or reflections on how these behaviors relate to your own experience. Allow yourself to observe and absorb both the factual information and your internal response. Such dual awareness is crucial to full integration and inner healing.

WHY DO THEY DO THIS?

Gaslighting is fundamentally a manipulative behavior. People manipulate because they want to "win" or achieve their objective more than they value the personhood of others.

Many people manipulate out of insecurity. Their objective may, at its core, be good, but they lack the confidence or social skills to assert their needs and wants or to grow relationships in healthy ways. Their fear of abandonment or of being unloved overshadows the embrace of healthy relationship patterns.

Some people gaslight out of an excessively felt need to get their way, attempting to fill self-esteem needs by dominating others. They may be so focused on image that they are willing to manipulate others into being in a relationship with them, because they can't accept rejection or the optics of being alone. They lack the courage to be vulnerable and risk rejection, and so they pursue control instead. Some care only about personal objectives and fail to see others as independent beings. Such dynamics are glaring warning signs of a toxic relationship.

MANIPULATIVE BEHAVIORS

Let's take a look at some of the specific tactics gaslighters employ. Keep in mind that, depending on the type of gaslighter and the depth of their pathology, not all ploys may be evident. Many gaslighters keep you feeling off-balance with compliments and grand gestures, only to turn around and undermine your trust with tactics such as these.

LYING, EXAGGERATING, OR MISREPRESENTING THE TRUTH

Gaslighters are pathological liars. Gaslighters lie in many ways and for ostensibly different purposes but always with the goal of maintaining psychological control. They may deny their behavior, both to you and to outsiders: *"I never hit you! I would never hit you." "She fell. She's so clumsy."* Such denials protect the sadistic or defensive gaslighter.

They may lie to get attention, particularly the narcissistic types. Some gaslighters tell grandiose lies, inflating their successes: "I had the highest marks the university has ever seen!" They may borrow celebrity, claiming and exaggerating associations with famous people. Some may invent victimhood to garner sympathy and attention, while deflecting from their failures: "No one has ever been more persecuted than I."

When unlikely stories pile up, it becomes impossible to determine when to trust the liar and when not to. You are conditioned to be wary of your own intuition and to trust the untrustworthy gaslighter.

Gaslighters seize upon innocuous occurrences to color their exaggerated stories. A small grease fire in a pan becomes a kitchen in flames. The exaggeration may be obvious, but as you let the hyperbole slide without questioning, the gaslighter is empowered. Each success at presenting their altered reality secures their dominance as one who will not be challenged. As the story is repeated, you may even begin to picture the memory more in line with the narrative, the flames shooting ever higher.

These are the dual goals of gaslighting lies: First, such brazen falsehoods test the limits of what you will accept. Simultaneously, they establish what you will accept by pushing that boundary ever further. Some people describe living with a gaslighter as drinking from a fire hose of lies. They come so rapidly that you don't have time to examine one before being knocked over by the next. This off-balancing effect is the goal.

MAKING HARMFUL COMPARISONS AND UNDERMINING YOUR ACCOMPLISHMENTS

Every time Quentin shared news of a recent accomplishment with his mother, the conversation turned immediately to something his brother had done. The same thing happened when he shared vulnerable feelings. His mother always responded with examples of how much harder his brother had it. She never denied his stories; she simply moved on, shifting attention. Quentin found himself resenting his brother, with a boiling anger that he guiltily tried to suppress. He wondered whether he had any right to feel bad after all, or whether his accomplishments were truly worthy of celebration.

Gaslighters may undermine your accomplishments by comparing them to something purportedly greater, minimizing their significance, or shifting attention away. Narcissistic gaslighters compulsively turn attention back toward themselves by performing, bragging, or storytelling in such a way as to highlight some aspect of their self-perceived greatness, or at times, their misfortune.

Such control of the narrative allows the gaslighter to maintain the upper hand in the covert power game. You are left continually desiring more of the gaslighter's attention and affirmation, a prize tantalizingly near, yet constantly just out of reach. Your need for their affirmation feeds the gaslighter's ego and keeps the "ball in their court." As long as you don't yet have what you so desire, you will keep coming back for more—or so they assume.

HOW THEY TALK ABOUT OTHERS

Whenever Nathan's father lost his temper and hit his brother, Nigel, their mother would comment when tucking Nathan in at night that she was sorry the day had been unpleasant due to Nigel's bad mood. Nathan trusted his gentle, sweet-natured mother, but these soothing words troubled him somehow in a way he couldn't explain. He nodded, accepting the underlying premise: Dad is good, Nigel is bad. But when he glanced over at the sleeping face of his younger brother in the bed next to his, he felt vaguely guilty.

Gaslighters frequently point to the moods of others to deflect away from their own behavior. In Nathan's and Nigel's home, the mother gaslit Nathan by emphasizing his brother's attitude, to deflect from the adult's responsibility to control himself. In her codependence, she gaslit the witness of physical abuse to protect the perpetrator.

If you suspect that someone is a gaslighter, observe for yourself how they speak about others and whether their narratives match your observations. Do you feel gaslit as they describe people you know? Trust your gut.

Gaslighters show a glimpse of their nature in how they talk about other people. Although gossiping, labeling, and name-calling are not the sole domain of gaslighters, they *are* warning signs. If they are speaking in distorted, contemptuous, and negative ways about others, you can assume that they likely do the same about you.

This behavior serves the gaslighter in two ways. First, it gives them power over the narrative by racing ahead to assert definitions of reality, a tactic that may override your own perceptions. When gaslighters target your sense of sanity, they chip away at your trust in your own awareness, influencing you to accept a distorted reality. Second, it allows them to externalize problems by blaming others for conflicts and letting themselves off the hook. If someone else is being "irrational," then the gaslighter can't be at fault.

HOW THEY TALK ABOUT YOU IN FRONT OF OTHERS

LaTasha didn't have to wonder what her colleagues said about her behind her back. Years of microaggressions had socialized her to project an even temperament. She also learned from her mother to be proud of her legacy of strength, that she was a free woman who did not need to accept oppression. So when she spoke up for herself or raised objections on a project—calmly, firmly, confidently—it was maddening to hear colleagues tell her not to be "angry," to "calm down," and not to be "irrational."

Labels like the ones LaTasha received are a way to dismiss the validity of the speaker's message. They return control to the dominant party and frequently reinforce oppressive norms at the expense of those being gaslit. Gaslighters may tell embarrassing or private stories about you in front of friends or make condescending jokes while excusing their actions as "only joking." Despite scoffing at your emotions when alone with you, they may exaggerate your emotions when talking about you to others. Many wield armchair diagnoses as a weapon, labeling those they seek to diminish and control as mentally ill. They refer to you in diminutive ways that reveal their biases, calling adult men "boys" or adult women "girls" or using racial slurs. You are left flustered and angry and labeled (and perhaps feeling) "overreactive" or "too sensitive." Gaslighters may even tell outright lies about you in front of others, knowing that your protests will be doubted.

Not only do these tactics cause emotional distress, but they also alienate you from your support system. This is critical to maintain and conceal psychological abuse. Your own embarrassment or shame may cause you to withdraw from these friends or family, and those hearing the stories or labels shared by the often-charming gaslighter may pull away in reaction to what they are led to believe.

INTIMIDATION

Gaslighters frequently employ intimidation to maintain control. This may involve implied or concrete threats, typically paired with discounting, mocking, or blaming you for your fearful reaction. A boyfriend might make a sudden punching gesture toward his partner, then laugh or angrily attack them for having the audacity to believe he would follow through. *"You know I've never hit you. Don't act like I'm some sort of abuser."* Because no physical contact is made, the partner rationalizes that the relationship may not be perfect, but it certainly isn't abusive.

The gaslighter may engage in such acts of intimidation out of legitimately uncontrolled anger. In these cases, the gaslighting is used to deflect away from their internal shame. Alternatively, it may be a calculated act, intentionally crafted to manipulate and maintain control. Intimidation may involve actual physical harm, with the threat of recurrence constantly lingering in the air between you.

Such abuses set up the welcome "honeymoon" trauma-bonding stage of caregiving and reconciliation, all part of the cycle of doubt-inspiring control. In this stage, the gaslighter becomes apologetic, and you are subliminally assigned the role of reassuring them that they are not a bad person. Intimidation further reduces the likelihood that you will confront them about their distortions, making it easier for them to escape taking responsibility.

NEVER TAKING RESPONSIBILITY

The day after her first date with Wyatt, Mara was sore and confused. She remembered being excited to go out with him and how their chemistry felt electric. She also remembered him refilling her drink again and again. In his charming, flirtatious way, Wyatt had pressed her further than she had wanted to go. The details were fuzzy, but she knew things did not end the way she wanted. Despite his words of "you know you want it," Mara was certain that she had not wanted it at all.

As these memories swirled in her head, the text message arrived. "Hey, Sexy. Had a great time last night. Wanted to make sure you got home okay. Call me." Mara stared at her phone. How could the same person who had so insistently violated her personal and sexual boundaries last night act as though everything were okay?

Gaslighters never take responsibility. They may deny fault, shift blame, or paint a rosy picture of a shared experience. You are manipulated to doubt and ignore your own memories. With the gaslighter's signature charm and confidence, you begin to wonder whether what they are projecting may be what actually happened, or whether you remembered it wrong. Refusing to take responsibility enables gaslighters to continually be let off the hook.

If confronted, gaslighters tend to use one of three tactics. They may react in rage, shifting to intimidation tactics. In so doing, they immediately restore their control while deflecting from their wrongdoing.

Conversely, the gaslighter may play the victim, centering themselves within the narrative. This is a common dynamic when a minority calls out someone's racist remark, and the offender shifts the focus to their own feelings about being called out. Likewise, the spouse caught having an affair may center their own feelings at not being immediately trusted again. "I can't believe you would accuse me of that!" is a common gaslighter's response.

Alternatively, they may attack your credibility, suggesting that you are hysterical, while remaining calm, suave, and aloof. When you become understandably distressed, the narrative that they are the stable and sane one is reinforced. Thus, they need never admit wrongdoing, and their narcissistic ego is protected and even reinforced.

SPLITTING AND TRIANGULATION

Splitting occurs when someone divides two connected parties and controls communication between them to manipulate outcomes. One parent may tell their child that the other parent has confided that they think she is a pest, then tell the other parent that the child wishes they would give her more space. Conversely, in what is referred to as triangulation, a manipulator may inappropriately draw a third person into what ought to be direct communication between two people, entangling them in the dysfunction.

The gaslighter's primary strategy is to cultivate and present a version of reality that benefits them. Consequently, any ally who might support their target's sense of reality must be separated from them. Gaslighters engage in splitting and triangulation to play involved parties against one another and to reinforce their position. When these strategies are successful, the problematic dynamics appear to be between the two targets, and attention is shifted away from the puppeteering of the gaslighter. In addition, when friction and distance enter the relationship between the two parties, the gaslighter emerges victorious as the apparently more trustworthy confidant.

Unhealthy parents may engage in such games with their children or with a child and their spouse. Narcissistic leaders may pit employees against one another. In larger social dynamics, a political party may play two elements of the alternative political party against each other to introduce confusion, distraction, and disorder. Regardless of the dynamic in which it occurs, this tactic has consistent aims: to control and to emerge as the "good guy."

ENTITLEMENT

Sadistic and narcissistic gaslighters approach the world with a sense of entitlement. They view themselves as rightfully sitting atop a hierarchy of dominance. Their actions serve to reinforce and maintain such valued supremacy.

Entitlement may be displayed in myriad ways. Many such people expect that they should be the one to get the job regardless of superior work ethic or effort. They frequently expect adoration and sex as often as desired without concern for the wants of the other person. They may demand that their romantic partners meet impossible standards of physical beauty even while failing to hold themselves to similar standards. They often demand cooperation, respect, and obedience from children without showing themselves worthy of respect, relying on positional authority. When such expectations are not fulfilled, they pivot rapidly to rage, force, or coercion.

Many such people borrow authority from religious or historical texts to reinforce their control and present their entitlement as a shared value. They may highlight the writings of early political leaders, appealing to your shared sense of patriotism, or quote scriptures, entangling you to accept their intended outcome. A religious sadistic or narcissistic gaslighter may demand or force a sexual encounter with his partner, then cite scriptures that exhort wives not to deny their husbands sex, or gaslight children into accepting physical punishment as normal by emphasizing scriptures that highlight obedience.

In this way, your intuitive awareness of having been violated, assaulted, or betrayed becomes muddied by conflicting loyalties: to self, partner, parent, or leader and to your own principles. Your intuition that something is wrong in the relationship is overwritten by cherished values. You are left to conclude that the other person is not to blame, but that if only you did better, all would be well. The gaslighting serves to reinforce the gaslighter's established sense of entitled superiority.

EVERYTHING HAS A COST

As with entitlement, such people are unlikely to give without expecting something in return. A date may expect sex if they paid for dinner. A parent may use a favor done previously as leverage to guilt you into time spent together.

Although reciprocity is a mark of a healthy relationship, such mental record keeping and use of past favors to manipulate outcomes is a useful tactic to the gaslighter. Ultimately, the gaslighter shifts attention from your wants, needs, and feelings to their own; seeds feelings of guilt; and twists circumstances to their own ends. There is a distinct lack of mutuality, as the favor isn't given freely but is part of a calculated maneuver for selfish gain.

Signs of a Healthy Relationship

Just as it is important to recognize the signs and signals of gaslighting, it is equally vital to create a vision of what a healthy relationship looks like. Let's look at some guiding principles to assess the quality of your close relationships and to help you frame standards for what you want in a relationship.

- Honesty and integrity are core values upheld by both.
- Each person is free to speak for themselves and to be heard.
- Care and empathy are mutually shared (yet no one is expected to fix the emotions of the other person).
- There is mutual openness to considering new perspectives. You can disagree.
- Both parties share equally in decision-making.
- Respect and support flow in both directions, rather than downstream.
- When compromise is necessary, sacrifice is shared.
- When one party hurts the other, they apologize sincerely, naming and taking responsibility for what they did.
- Both feel physically safe.
- There is commitment to continual growth, which may involve change.

THE POWER OF NAMING WHAT'S HAPPENING TO YOU

As you read and reflect on these tactics, what resonates? Do you feel a dawning recognition or "aha" sense, an inner resistance, or a sense of clarity? Do you feel excitement at finally starting to make sense of your confusion and frustration, a sense of vindication, or anger in recognizing what's really going on?

You have probably heard the idiom that "knowledge is power," and especially in this context, it's true. In making sense of what has been happening, you are taking the first step to changing the dynamic, taking back your power, and improving your life. When you can identify and label what's being done to you, you become empowered to fight back effectively and make decisions about what you will accept in your life. When you realize that it really is them, not you, you become free.

In the next chapter, we will dive more deeply and broadly into understanding emotional abuse, how it impacts you, and what healing can look like. Healing is possible. Freedom awaits.

CHAPTER 3:
EMOTIONAL ABUSE AND RECOVERY

Whether you suspect or have already determined that you have suffered gaslighting, it's a good idea to consider how else emotional abuse may be affecting your life. In this chapter, we will explore what emotional abuse is, where it happens, and how it impacts you. From there, we will begin to explore how to break away from such corrosive influences and begin to heal.

EMOTIONAL ABUSE

Emotional abuse is psychological harm inflicted without requisite physical contact. It includes verbal abuse and name-calling, manipulation, bullying, threatening, shaming, constant criticism, withholding affection, and isolating the target. While emotional abuse can occur separately from physical harms like physical or sexual abuse, it is also a constant companion of such abuses. Emotional abuse results in psychological scarring, reflected in depression, anxiety, PTSD, or personality disorders. Emotional attacks may happen impulsively or be orchestrated intentionally with a consistent and targeted aim of control.

Gaslighting is one form of emotional abuse. It commonly accompanies other patterns of emotional abuse, either working together toward a uniform goal or covering up for explosive, unplanned verbal or physical abuse. As with all emotional abuse, it curtails independence by controlling through attacking your self-confidence.

It may be hard to identify specific examples in your own life to pinpoint whether emotional abuse is present. For many, it is an experience likened to "death by a thousand cuts," with the evidence embedded in the effects. Emotional abuse leaves you feeling depressed, tense, drained, unworthy, and like you are not "enough."

For many people, it can be difficult to admit that they have experienced emotional abuse. A common refrain I hear from hurting individuals, unsure why they can't just get over their symptoms, is "but it's not like I was _____." It can be so hard to face the fact that we have experienced real harm without diminishing our pain by comparing it with that of others. But scaling pain does no one any favors, nor does it reduce its effects; it only limits your ability to heal.

Many people deny emotional abuse to resist feeling like a victim. And that instinct can be good: There is an internal fighter in you who won't submit. That internal fighter helped protect your spirit through the worst of it. But perhaps today it is time to thank your inner fighter for its help and let it rest for a bit. Allow the hurt child to speak their truth.

Another powerful reason people resist calling out the emotional abuse in their life is to protect their loved one. Because truly, no one can hurt us on this deep level as much as someone we love. These aren't attacks from a stranger. This is probably someone who matters to you a lot. But such denial protects them only at your expense. By denying what has happened or is happening, you allow the fault to remain where they have placed it: on you. If they are without fault, you are broken. And if they are exonerated, you have no right to place limits, create distance, or cultivate a healthier dynamic. There can be no change.

You deserve better. I don't need to have met you to know this. You are intrinsically worthy of love and respect.

Gaslighting and emotional abuse don't happen exclusively in romantic relationships.

Bosses may change project expectations and criticize you for following original expectations or shame you in front of colleagues. They may engage in sexual harassment, deny the behavior, then label you as inappropriately flirtatious in the work-place. Friends may manipulate through vague complaints of being ignored to create guilt and seek affection indirectly rather than asking for time together, then become enraged when their needs aren't met. Parents may criticize, belittle, and shame their children, while insisting that they are a happy family or that the only prob-lem is the child's presumed mental illness.

Because emotional abuse and gaslighting happen in various contexts, the effects are likewise varied. The higher the number of such people in your life, the greater the psychological toll. The closer the abuser is to you and the greater the degree to which you depend upon them, the more difficult it can be to both rec-ognize and escape or change the dynamics. But take heart! It can be done.

Does This Sound Like You?

If you are uncertain whether you have experienced emo-tional abuse, consider the common outcomes. If many of these effects sound familiar, particularly in the absence of other traumas, it's likely that you have.

- Self-doubt
- Shame
- Feeling like you are either "not enough" or "too much"
- Self-criticism/negative internal voice
- Feelings of worthlessness
- Disordered eating
- Addictive behaviors (substances, shopping, food, gambling)

- Heightened need for affirmation/reassurance
- Avoidance of intimacy
- Anxiety
- Depression
- Hopelessness and suicidal thoughts

*If you are experiencing suicidal thoughts, please call the National Suicide Prevention Lifeline at **800-273-8255** (in the United States) or the Canada Suicide Prevention Service at **833-456-4566** (in Canada).*

WHAT IT DOES TO YOU

Many people are tempted to dismiss emotional abuse because it leaves no physical scars. Yet its effects are far-reaching and profound. Emotional abuse is, in its essence, the undermining of your self-esteem and independence. Low self-regard and shame are foundational to depression and social anxiety.

Emotional abuse undermines secure attachment, a core human need. Although the physical necessities of food, water, clothing, and shelter keep us alive, attachment allows us to thrive. We cannot choose not to need or be impacted by others, and gaslighting preys upon exactly that fundamental, basic need. Insecure attachment leads us to cling excessively to unhealthy relationships or avoid closeness altogether.

From infancy, our brains are primed to co-regulate with others through "mirror neurons" that allow us to perceive and feel what others are feeling. Babies and young children who are consistently exposed to soothing caregivers internalize such responses, and the experience of finding calm and contentedness shapes the developing brain. Those continually exposed to chaos or yelling, or who are ignored, fail to develop internal regulation and are at heightened risk of developing anxiety disorders later in life.

When we are constantly exposed to anger, even in adulthood, our brains strengthen the neural pathways associated with fear and danger. Constant exposure to criticism neurologically reinforces shame, hopelessness, and sadness as well. Just as plants exposed to angry music wither, we also flourish or flounder based on the emotional tone of our environments.

It is frequently said that children are resilient. This may be true, but it does not mitigate the impacts of abuse or trauma. Wounds are incorporated into their developing psyches, which continue to influence actions and reactions in adulthood. One way we adapt to living in an environment of constant assaults, whether as children or adults, is to assimilate it as normal. We may find that we no longer think of it as unusual anymore.

But even when we repress the truth of what is happening to us, the body knows. Emotional abuse takes a physical toll, leading to a higher probability of physical ailments, ranging from gastrointestinal distress to autoimmune disorders to cancer. Research by the Kaiser Foundation, which included over 17,000 participants, demonstrated that the more adverse childhood events experienced—including emotional abuse—the higher the likelihood of a wide range of physical illnesses in adulthood.

Such sobering findings highlight the importance of taking emotional abuse seriously. What is minimized and ignored cannot be healed, and what remains unresolved can lead to serious negative outcomes both psychosocially and physically. However, what is acknowledged can be addressed, and healing can begin, lessening such serious effects.

PHYSICAL ABUSE

If your relationship crosses the threshold where anger turns to violence, reach out. Seek help. This is not normal or okay. Physical abuse always escalates over time and may become lethal. You do not deserve this. Staying will not pacify or fix things. Call for help today.

USA: National Domestic Violence Hotline: 800-799-SAFE (7233)

TTY: 800-787-3224

Canada: Canadian Resource Centre for Victims of Crime: 877-232-2610

Text: 613-208-0747

Amira dreaded the moment her husband would walk through the door. Without greeting her, Aaron would slam the door, light a cigarette, and demand his dinner—which had to be ready when he arrived. The children were expected to have put away their toys and be bathed, fed, and out of sight. If any of these expectations were not met, Aaron berated Amira as a lousy failure.

As she watched Aaron eat dinner in stony silence, Amira's mind flashed back to her childhood and her own beloved father yelling at her mother over a spot on the teapot. She remembered shyly bringing him a flower she had picked, and his quick glance at it before tossing it on the table and asking whether she had obeyed her mother. She remembered how deflated she felt, yet grateful to have his attention as she assured him that she had been good.

Somehow it felt that no matter how hard she tried, then as now, she was never able to measure up. "I'm just not enough," Amira concluded.

One critical way that we adapt to emotional abuse is by internalizing shame. A child subjected to emotional abuse will not recognize that something is wrong with the parent's behavior. They must trust their parent in order to survive. Instead, they often internalize the message of the abuse, concluding that they themselves are to blame. They learn to hate not the abusive parent but themselves.

Emotional abuse is usually inconsistent. Harsh and continual criticism, shaming, cursing, and isolation or the "silent treatment" may be paired with times of fun, connection, and even messages of "I love you." When children experience love as involving emotional abuse, that defines their understanding of love.

Too often, this begins a pattern that persists throughout life. After a childhood saturated with harsh criticism, belittling, and anger, most people do not enter into warm, kind, or secure adult relationships. Rather, childhood emotional abuse primes you to normalize and accept similarly unhealthy dynamics in adult partnerships.

Likewise, those who abuse are generally reflecting patterns they themselves experienced in childhood. The abuser may have identified with the aggressor, failed to see the problem in the pattern, and internalized the harmful messages. Alternatively, they may not have absorbed self-regulation skills, due to a lack of modeling or extensions of comfort from parents when distressed, and so they continue the cycle in reactivity and shame.

While this is the usual pattern, there may be outliers. In certain cultures and belief systems, for example, women may be social-ized to be subservient, expect dominance (the cornerstone of abuse), and remain faithful to a relationship at any cost. Some become trapped by disabilities, threats to harm family members, or financial dependence.

Regardless of the psychological or other constraints that keep you bound, please know that you are worthy. You deserve uncon-ditional love.

TRAUMA AND COMPLEX PTSD

Perhaps you are someone who has experienced abusive relation-ships throughout your life, beginning in childhood. Such abuse constitutes not a singular trauma but a continual constellation of traumas. These are heightened in impact due to the timing of this critical developmental stage. As children grow, their brains are forming. Inadequate attachment impacts the developing brain, setting the groundwork for lifelong struggles with depres-sion and anxiety.

Growing up in fear likewise creates constant trauma expo-sure. The part of your nervous system responsible for regulating your calming reflexes or your fight-or-flight reactions becomes strained from overuse. This leads to two possible outcomes: your brain may strengthen neural pathways that reinforce anxious, hypervigilant reactions, or your self-preservative energy may become so depleted that you plummet into a state of exhausted depression without enough will or strength to protect yourself.

Trauma is the impact of an experience that overwhelms your natural ability to cope and assimilate what happened. It may result from witnessing a horrific event, such as a death or serious bodily injury to another, a near-death experience, or an assault on your bodily sovereignty, like a sexual assault. Complex trauma results when you are subjected to ongoing traumas, like living in a war zone or growing up with continual childhood abuse. Because such trauma occurs while the brain is forming and developing, it is also referred to as developmental trauma.

With fewer resources to cope with overwhelming experiences, children may develop dissociative defenses, effectively splitting off a part of their consciousness to escape the pain of the present reality. Depending on how strong the need to dissociate is, this can lead to lifelong experiences of feeling like multiple selves, or simply feeling disconnected from one's self and body. You may find it easy to separate your feelings from your factual knowledge of an event, while at other times being flooded by overwhelming anger or fear connected to triggering reminders of the trauma. Poor memory recall is common as well; when a person dissociates, it hampers communication between the various brain structures, while trauma shrinks the hippocampus, the region of the brain responsible for storing and retrieving long-term memory.

The good news is that the brain continues to grow, change, and adapt throughout life, a phenomenon called "neuroplasticity." This means that these impairments can change. The hippocampus can grow, improving memory. Traumatic memories can be adaptively processed and integrated into long-term memory, where they are not constantly demanding attention. You can learn and practice grounding techniques that will decrease dissociation in the present. Triggers can be identified and reprocessed with therapeutic approaches we will discuss in part 2. Healing is possible, and it can change your life.

ENGAGING WITH MULTIPLE ABUSERS

If you experienced emotional abuse and gaslighting in childhood and unhealthy relationships in adulthood, you may find yourself with multiple abusers in your life. You may be juggling the stresses of complicated relationships with your parents and siblings while navigating unhealthy or toxic dynamics in your romantic relationship or your friendships. A lifetime of gaslighting and emotional abuse can make it difficult to recognize unhealthy dynamics and set boundaries. Without these skills, you are more likely to keep friends in your life who don't treat you well, stay in jobs with narcissistic bosses, or even accept the unhealthy dynamics of cults. Such abuses pile on top of one another, each weight alone perhaps bearable, but together a crushing burden.

When unsatisfying and unsupportive relationships surround you, not only is the load extreme, but you may lack an adequate support system to help you carry the weight. Whom do you turn to when you need to vent or work through a problem if your brother is dismissive, your mother shames you, and your friends continually turn all attention to themselves? Where do you go when you're feeling overwhelmed by the impossible demands of your gaslighting boss if your partner labels your stress as hysterics? Where do you find solidarity amid the pressures of racism or sexism when you feel that no matter how loudly you speak, no one is listening?

This is a dark place to be. But you are not trapped by the past. Your future is not set based on your upbringing, trauma, or heritage. Healing and change are possible in your life. Hold on to hope. Press ahead. Let's explore how these cycles can be stopped.

HOW DO I HEAL?

You *can* heal from emotional abuse and gaslighting, no matter how long or from how many people you have suffered it. Healing means breaking the bonds of the experience and becoming free to choose new ways of feeling, thinking, and interacting that are not ordained by the past. It involves recognizing and admitting what happened or is happening, finding self-compassion, and growing in self-respect. It also means building confidence in your justified right and ability to establish healthy relationships and pursue the life you desire.

Recovery is a process. It doesn't happen all at once. It can feel, at times, like taking two steps forward, then one step back, but keep your eye on the goal, measuring long-term rather than short-term change. One day you will look back and be amazed and proud of how far you have come. For now, be patient with yourself and don't demand overnight change. Those harsh voices belong in the past.

THE 7 STEPS

Healing begins with *acceptance*. Before we can change a problem, we must recognize what it is and that it exists. You may have already gained a measure of acceptance as you worked through the initial chapters of this book. If so, take heart: healing has already begun!

The second step is to *understand the cycle*, which you also may be starting to recognize as you reflect on the tactics outlined in chapter 2. As you come to terms with these realities, allow yourself space for the third step, to *grieve* what is and what has been lost. This third step can be painful, but it can also be a much-needed release.

As you grieve, you move into the fourth step, allowing for *self-focus*. This is not selfishness; it's granting yourself the compassion that you have always deserved. It may feel foreign because it has been absent far too long. In this space of moving inward, deep healing can emerge.

The fifth step, *boundary setting*, allows you to cultivate a healthy space around you where you can grow and flourish. You begin to prune the vines or pull the weeds that have choked your health. Building upon these boundaries and reflecting upon the responses received, in the sixth step you *make decisions* about whom to allow in or remove from your life.

In the seventh and final step of healing, you begin to intentionally *develop new and healthy relationships*, with full awareness of what you want and deserve in a mutually respectful friendship, professional relationship, or loving partnership. Bringing with you the knowledge and awareness you have gained, building on the self-compassion you have fostered, and instituting firm yet kind boundaries that will protect you and allow you to love, your healing bears fruit as a new phase of your life begins. In this phase, you learn to break the cycle for good.

Go slowly as you move through these steps. Give yourself time, grace, and patience as you work toward healing these tender wounds. Rushing ahead may lead to frustration. Some steps may go more quickly than others. That's okay. You may find yourself revisiting former steps. That's okay, too. Be compassionate with your process as you progress toward change.

Know that the abuse was never your fault. Living with a gaslighter and suffering emotional abuse is not something you did wrong nor something to be ashamed of. The important thing now is that in acknowledging what has happened in your life, you can create the necessary space you need to heal.

In the pages ahead, I will break down these seven steps even further to make them practical and tangible. Before you turn that next page, take some time to pause for a self-care moment of rest:

Put down this book. Stretch. Get a glass of water to drink. Look outside at something green for a full minute or more. Breathe deeply and slowly, noticing the rise and fall of your breath as it fills your lungs and nourishes your cells. Close your eyes and just notice whatever you are feeling. When you are ready, let's begin with the first step to freedom.

PART TWO
THE 7 STEPS

Now that we have established some fundamental concepts and clarified understanding of gaslighting and emotional abuse, let's begin the work of breaking those chains. If you have come to suspect or conclude that you have been dealing with gaslighting, you probably aren't satisfied allowing it to continue. I know that change is scary, but I also suspect that the fighter in you is what drove you to pick up this book.

In this second part, we will explore the seven steps to freedom from gaslighting. Through acceptance, understanding, grief, self-care, boundaries, decision-making, and developing new, healthy relationships, you can break the cycle for good.

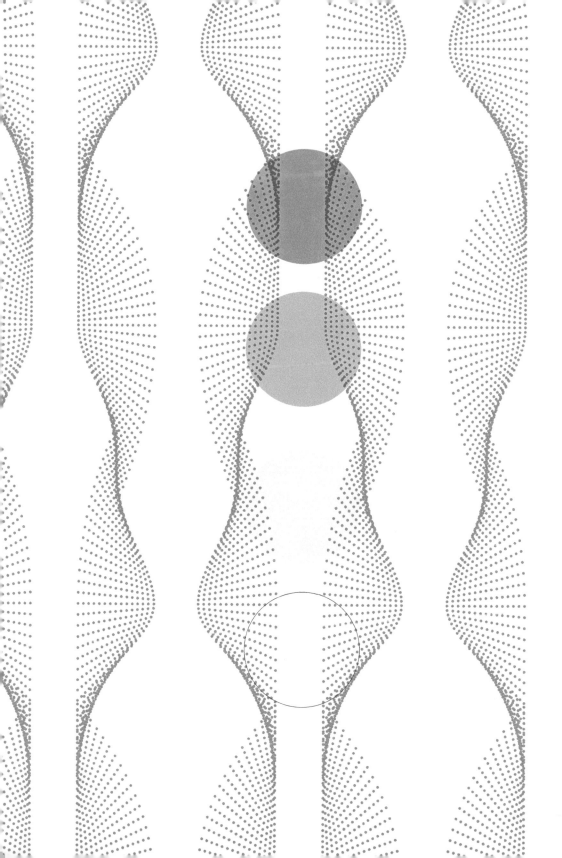

STEP 1:
ACCEPT THAT IT'S HAPPENING

The first step to breaking the chains of gaslighting and other emotional abuse is acceptance. Until you can recognize and accept the truth of what is happening to you, you remain vulnerable to its influence. Accepting the reality of what you have been living with empowers you to make a change.

DEFINING ACCEPTANCE

Acceptance does not mean that you are okay with what is or has happened to you. It does not mean accepting the behavior and allowing it to continue. It does not mean letting the person who has been hurting you "off the hook."

It *does* mean accepting the reality of the situation. Rather than denying, minimizing, or refusing to question, you turn toward the problem and assess it squarely. If the signs point toward such manipulative patterns, you accept this fact for what it is. Acceptance is recognition of reality.

In this first stage of acceptance, you do not attempt to change or fight against what is. Simply name it and allow yourself to feel the weight of it. Don't rush over this stage even if it feels like a simple admission to yourself. Mindfully acknowledge what is, and allow yourself awareness of the internal consequences and costs of its presence in your life.

This process is intrinsically complicated when dealing with gaslighting, which by nature causes you to doubt yourself and your feelings, perceptions, and experience. Gaslighting makes you feel like you are crazy and labels you as the one with the problem. This makes it challenging to untangle the knot of lies, distortions, and your own perceptions. Remember what we discussed in chapter 1: if you feel like you are being gaslit, you probably are.

The very act of picking up and reading this far into this book suggests that you have already begun—and made progress on—the process of acceptance.

ACCEPTANCE IS ESSENTIAL

Acceptance is essential to make change. You cannot change something you do not acknowledge, nor will you be committed to the process if you are unsure. You deserve to heal and to be free.

Acceptance begins with naming the problem. You stop rationalizing, making excuses, accepting blame, and explaining things away. This part can be painful. I won't pretend it is easy. Not only are you shifting paradigms and reanalyzing everything you thought you knew and experienced, but you may feel you are silently betraying someone you love or care about.

Yet love, whether between parent and child, romantic partners, or platonic friends, does not demand that you accept manipulation or abuse. Love does not hurt. Love does not demand that you absorb blow after blow. Healthy love has boundaries that protect and honor both parties.

Do you feel loved or respected? How often do you feel hurt? Does love or affirmation exist only in a cycle, as a follow-up to abuse? Do you take it as your job only to give, expecting nothing in return? Perhaps a lifetime of emotional abuse has trained you to expect nothing more, suggesting you don't deserve better. This is a lie.

Acceptance begins with noticing. Notice what you feel. Take time to listen to your inner voice, your intuition. Notice the patterns in your relationship, and pay attention to the feelings this brings up. In the noticing, honor your intuition by respecting this inner wisdom. Let it speak truth to you.

CHECK IN WITH YOURSELF

To survive emotional abuse, you may have learned to push your emotions deep down inside. Constant criticism, blaming, shaming, and verbal attacks cause such relentless, deep pain that responsive reactions like suppression, denial, and dissociation from your feelings may have been necessary to continue on. Gaslighting may have taught you that your feelings are histrionics—too much, too dramatic, a sign of being crazy or unreliable.

Now you stand at a crossroads. Will you continue to deny the impact of such abuse on your spirit? Or will you name it and allow yourself the grace of healing? "Tough" is not strong. Vulnerability is the true test of strength, because it requires immense strength to bear these emotions and feel all that you have buried for so long.

Begin to set aside a little time, perhaps several times daily, to check in with yourself. Ask yourself how you are truly feeling. This may feel uncomfortable or strange at first. Just go with it. Persist, allowing yourself to explore your own emotional landscape. Some of your feelings may be distressing or unpleasant. Just notice that, with gentle compassion. It is okay to feel. You are not crazy, and your emotions are not "too much." Feelings do not make you weak.

This process is essential as you are coming to accept the reality that you have been experiencing gaslighting and emotional abuse. It also creates a pause—small moments to notice, reflect, and choose. This grants you greater choice and control in your actions and reactions, so that as you gain awareness of your emotions, you also grow in mastery over them.

Take a moment now to try this. Settle into a comfortable place if you aren't in one already. Let the book rest on your lap or beside you. Close your eyes. Take a deep breath in through your nose, counting slowly to five. Hold the breath for a moment, then slowly release it as you count to six. Repeat this several times. Notice where your mind goes. Notice what you are feeling. Are you calm? Anxious? Irritated? Impatient? Relaxed? Confused? There is no wrong answer and no wrong way to feel.

Notice where you feel that emotion in your body. Where do you hold the tension? Are your shoulders tensed? Is your brow furrowed? Does your heart feel tight or your stomach clenched?

Now bring your attention back to your breath. Continue to breath in slowly, hold, and exhale slowly. As you breathe in, silently name the positive feeling you wish to receive. Perhaps the word is "peace," "serenity," "clarity," or "calm." As you exhale, silently and with intention name the negative feeling you wish to release: "Letting go of fear." "Releasing anger." Repeat this at least five times, or for as long as it feels right to you.

Notice what happens with the tension in your body. Bring your attention to a place in your body that feels strong, calm, or free of tension. Let your attention rest there.

As you practice this each day—perhaps upon waking, before going to bed, or anytime you notice an internal shift throughout the day—you begin to train yourself to recognize your feelings. Even more important, by practicing this awareness, you learn to value and validate your own emotions, a critical step to inner healing.

How Am I Feeling?

If tuning in to your emotions is new to you, here are some simple questions to get you started:

- What am I feeling in my body right now?
- Do these feelings seem connected to any emotions?
- Has anything happened today that was upsetting to me?
- If so, what happened?
- What word pops to mind that describes my feelings about it?

- Do I want to shift my mood?
- If so, what do I want to feel?
- What is one thing I could do that might help me feel that way?

It is so important to be honest with yourself. You have been lied to and manipulated, likely for a significant amount of time, by someone else, maybe someone you love. This can be painful to admit. You do not deserve this. You can honor your right to truth and honesty by giving it to yourself.

When you have been continually manipulated in this way, your sense of reality may feel fragile and uncertain, your foundation shaken. This can make you feel crazy, but you're not.

Because abusers isolate their targets, they may be your only support system. This makes it frightening to accept and hard to stay objective—where do you go if your "safe place" isn't safe?

Being hurt by someone you love can also affect your self-worth. Please know you are *not* to blame and you did not bring this upon yourself. They may not see all the beauty and value in you, but that doesn't *diminish* its truth. Your worth is immutable and intrinsic.

As you are honest with yourself, affirming the truths that you know, you begin to build a solid foundation in this place of shifting sand. You can recognize and reject the lies that assail you. Being true to yourself is the first step to reclaiming your power, your sense of self, and your emotional well-being.

Mantras/Affirmations for Acceptance

When you have endured gaslighting and emotional abuse, it is so easy to internalize shame. Repeating or meditating on mantras or affirmations such as these can help shift your critical self-talk to a voice of confidence and embolden you to reject the gaslighter's manipulations.

- I am enough.
- I deserve love.
- I am worthy.
- I am allowed to take up space.
- My feelings matter.
- I trust my inner wisdom.
- I am wonderful just the way that I am.
- I am filled with divinity/I bear the image of God.

IDENTIFY THE ABUSER'S TACTICS

Since childhood, Phillip had taken many psychotropic medications as his mother focused on finding a mental illness to explain away his fluctuating emotions. He began his university years with an embedded belief that he was chronically broken.

Nevertheless, Phillip grew tired of the medications' side effects and decided to try life without them. He worried that he would start to have psychotic episodes, as his mother had warned, but he didn't. Instead, he was thriving, joining the swim team, and dating a caring young man.

As Phillip's relationship with his boyfriend, Leonard, grew, he slowly began to share stories of life with his mother. One day, Leonard suggested that his mother may have been gaslighting him. Was it possible, he wondered, that his mother had dragged him to therapists until she found one willing to accept her desired assessment and prescribe the sedatives so useful for control?

As he re-examined his childhood, Phillip realized the tantrums and crying spells that had been pointed to as signs of mental illness were natural responses in a sensitive boy living with a controlling, critical, and at times explosively angry mother. Rather than listen to his hurt, his mother found a doctor willing to medicate him for a severe illness that would bring her sympathy and deflect away any fault on her part.

It was painful for Phillip to accept. And yet, as he stood fast in his dawning understanding, pushing back on her continual attempts to focus on the pathology he never had, Phillip felt strong for the first time.

The gaslighting in Phillip's life was insidious and lifelong, making it difficult to identify. His natural adolescent dependence on his mother made it hard to recognize and call out the abusive behavior. Because he was so immersed in it, he internalized the shame, feeling helpless and worthless. Had he never gained space and the support of an outside view to re-examine this relationship, he might never have stopped the cycle.

Taking an objective stance is vital to identifying and labeling the tactics for what they are. If you have experienced years of gaslighting, outside perspectives like those provided by Phillip's boyfriend may be essential to helping you sort through the pieces of your experience, critically examining them. If this trustworthy person has known you throughout the relationship in question, their insight may be of even greater value, because they may be able to validate memories you have come to doubt.

This book can also serve in that capacity as an objective partner in your quest. Using the discussions of tactics commonly used in chapter 2, hold your experiences up as though to a mirror and see what you find reflected there.

Journal your thoughts, writing fluidly without censoring yourself or stopping to read what you have written (until you are done). Try writing with your nondominant hand. It will be messy, but this switch will tap into your more intuitive mental processes, as your usual language-producing actions are linked with the logical hemisphere of your brain. This will help you move beyond self-censorship if you are feeling stuck. Then go back and read your writing with an analytical eye.

NAME SPECIFIC SITUATIONS

Phillip's story presents just one example of obstacles to recognition and acceptance. You may have been told that you are "just being dramatic," are "being selfish," or are "tearing the family apart" with your "lies." Such accusations serve to silence you and cause you to doubt your emerging self-knowledge and situational awareness. Recognizing and labeling these suppression tactics for what they are can help you stand strong in the truth.

As you begin to gain confidence and name what is happening, unexpected and mysterious triggers become comprehensible. You may have times of strong emotional reactions and anger toward the other person, and perhaps you aren't fully aware of why that is. Being able to label what is happening helps you regain control internally. As you recognize the cycle of manipulative tactics, you become freer to step outside the game. Instead of being brushed aside as something imaginary, your pain makes sense.

When you suspect that perhaps you are being gaslit, note that to yourself, or even say it aloud. "I think I am being gaslit here." Take a step back and examine the specific situation. Gather more information if necessary, by asking questions, calling out what you know, or asking witnesses what they perceived. This will empower you to separate from the "crazy cycle" and decide consciously how to respond.

For example, if you suspect that your partner is cheating and gaslighting you to cover up, or that your colleague is gaslighting you to mask evidence of their corruption, make a list of the scenarios that cause you doubt and the explanations they have provided. Write it all down without stopping to rationalize or reason with any instance. Then, when it is all out on paper, read it over with an objective eye. Reread your journal entries from those days to compare notes. Perhaps share your lists with a trusted friend or therapist for an outside perspective.

Trust your intuition. Decide where or how you need more information to confirm suspicions, rather than running from your fears. The truth may be painful for a time, but it can set you free from the ongoing hurt of anxious wondering.

YOU ARE NOT TO BLAME

As you begin to accept what is happening in your relationship, please hold on to this fundamental truth: you are not to blame. No matter how messy the interactions, no matter what dynamics

are at play, the responsibility for lying, manipulating, and gaslighting remains squarely on the one who has been doing it.

Perhaps you know this intellectually, but the truth has not yet settled in your heart. For now, work on trusting what you know. Conviction takes time. It is so common when you have experienced trauma to have a disconnect between what you feel and what you know, because trauma blocks normal processing and locks thoughts and feelings away in their separate brain regions. If you get stuck here, there are powerful brain-based therapies and tools we will discuss later that can help you deeply integrate the truths you know but don't yet feel.

Accepting that you are not to blame can be particularly challenging when dealing with gaslighters, because their behavior is inherently devised to avoid accepting responsibility. Their game is crafted to shift blame onto you and make you accept this distortion. To break free, you must recognize the power play and reject it. You must accept that you are not at fault for the gaslighting or the behavior it is designed to conceal.

COMING TO TERMS

Acceptance may not be a smooth, linear process. You may have moments when you feel a rush of conviction, clarity, or even anger. The next day you may be mired again in doubt.

Go back to your journal. Reread what you have written and reflect on it. Close your eyes, feel your feelings, and listen to your inner voice of wisdom.

As you gain clarity and understanding, you may begin to feel a sense of peace. There may be sadness and anger, too, but the confusion will begin to melt away into a calm confidence. You don't have to make decisions yet, but you have begun to make a change, simply in the knowing. Your newfound or growing clarity is the start of the process that will free you.

To help internalize acceptance, try the following exercises. Use what is helpful to you in the space you are in.

EXERCISE 1: CONNECTING THE DOTS

This exercise, adapted from acceptance and commitment therapy (ACT), helps clarify realities that you may be avoiding. Grab a journal to write down your responses.

- First, list the thoughts, feelings, fears, and memories you may be avoiding—anything you can think of that may be associated with gaslighting and emotional abuse in your relationship.
- Second, identify the **DOTS**:
  - **D:** What **distractions** do you engage in to avoid thinking of these things? (for example, television, shopping, gossip, social media)
  - **O:** What have you **opted out** of to avoid them? (perhaps conversations, confrontations, or relationships)
  - **T:** How have you changed your **thinking** to avoid these truths? (using processes like rationalization, denial, or minimization)
  - **S:** What **substances** or other **self-harming** activities have you used to avoid thoughts and feelings about what is happening? (such as alcohol, binge eating, self-mutilation)
- Finally, consider how this avoidance has served or harmed you. Where would you be today if you removed the DOTS and allowed yourself to explore the truth? (Would you have sought out a job promotion, cultivated new friendships, experienced better health?)

EXERCISE 2: TAPPING IN WITH THE EMOTIONAL FREEDOM TECHNIQUE

This exercise is based on the principles of acupressure, which uses tapping on key pressure points, combined with an acceptance mantra.

- Note the intensity of your distress about the gaslighting/emotional abuse on a scale of 0 to 10.
- Tap with two fingers on your eyebrow while repeating the following:

"Even though I don't like what's been happening, I deeply and completely accept myself."

- Continue this process, moving the tapping to the outside of the eye, the bone below the eye, under the nose, on the chin, on the collarbone, on the underarm, and finishing on the crown of the head, repeating the words in each position.
- Reassess your level of distress. Continue this process until you feel a greater sense of calm and self-acceptance in the midst of the situation.

EXERCISE 3: CREATING CALM

This exercise helps you develop personal resources and coping skills to aid in the process of accepting painful truths and emotions.

- List five specific things that give you a sense of peace. Consider all your senses. For example, the smell of a specific scented candle or essential oil, the feel of petting your cat, the sound of a soothing music track, or the taste of herbal tea.

1. _____

   _____

2. _____

   _____

3. _____

_____

4. _____

_____

5. _____

_____

- Practice using these sensory calming aids not to avoid but to assist in moving through feelings evoked by your emotionally abusive relationship. As you cultivate the ability to create inner calm, you realize that you can accept painful truths without being overcome.

Now that you have begun to accept the reality of what is happening in your relationship, let's deepen that awareness by exploring typical patterns that relationships with gaslighters follow. As you deepen your understanding of what is transpiring in your life, you become increasingly empowered to break those chains.

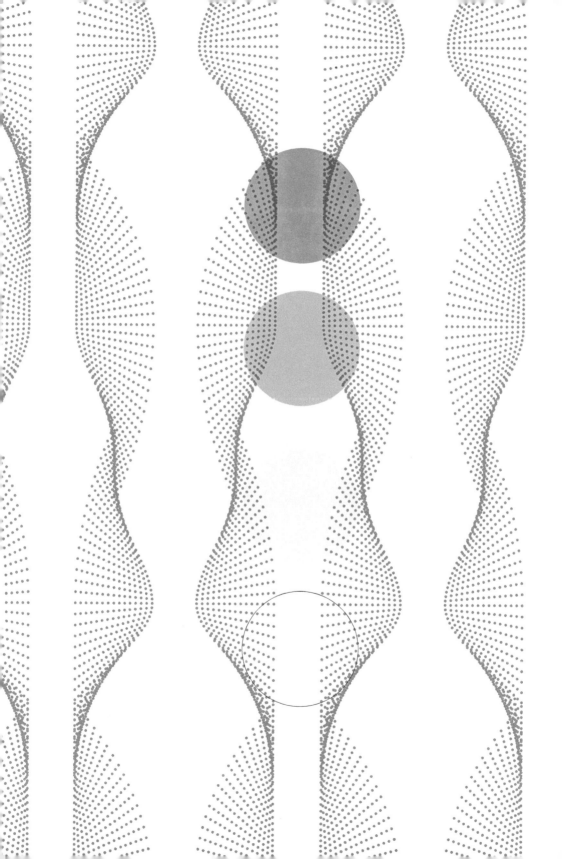

STEP 2:
UNDERSTAND THE CYCLE

To break free from gaslighting, it helps to understand the cycles. As you learn about these common behavioral patterns, you may find that some have a ring of familiarity to them, while others may not connect with your experience.

As you read each one, notice what comes up for you. Notice how your body reacts, and be open to what your body's response is telling you. Even as you identify your own wounds, you are learning what to resist in the future. This empowers you to protect yourself from harm and remain open only to those relationships that will be life-giving to you.

RELATIONSHIP PATTERNS

There are several common patterns in relationships with gaslighters. As we explore these, keep in mind that not every relationship follows every pattern. The macabre dance between gaslighter and target depends on the pathology and type of gaslighter involved, whether sadistic, narcissistic, or defensive.

LOVE-BOMBING, DEVALUING, DISCARDING

Angelina was thrilled by the attention of her boss, Rose, a strong, successful, and influential journalist. It was validating to receive Rose's praise and attention, lunch invitations, and consideration for exciting assignments. Rose even hinted that Angelina might sit at her desk one day.

Angelina noticed that Rose could be brusque at times. She tried to brush off Rose's cutting comments on her style of dress, even changing her wardrobe to more closely mimic Rose's own. When Rose gave scathing feedback on her writing, tossing it back in full view of Angelina's colleagues, Angelina told herself it was the price of mentorship, with Rose intermittently telling her how she just wanted Angelina to fulfill her potential.

While Angelina's work quality increased, the negative feedback escalated. It became harder to brush off comments such as "Can't you do anything right?" or "Did you write this or did your dog?" Angelina was crushed when she saw Rose invite another intern to lunch, a privilege Angelina alone had shared. As they walked from the room, she overheard Rose saying, "I want to talk to you about your future with the company. You have so much potential . . ."

Not long after that, Angelina was called into Rose's office and handed a termination slip releasing her from her at-will internship. Angelina fought back tears as she read it. When she looked up, Rose stated, "That is all. You may go." Angelina left in disgrace.

Angelina's work experience illustrates the cycle of love-bombing followed by devaluation and culminating in discarding of the target. Before we break this cycle down further, let's consider it from another angle in the romantic relationship of Lin and Erich.

Lin met Erich in the pouring rain after her night class let out. As Lin stood helplessly next to her flat tire, Erich's approach was a welcome sight, as was his invitation to wait in his car while he changed her tire.

Charmed by his gallantry, Lin jumped at his invitation to warm up at a nearby café, and the relationship progressed quickly. Erich seemed too good to be true; handsome and *attentive, he showered her with compliments. She found it cute that he seemed jealous when other guys noticed her.*

Although Lin wanted to move slowly with their physical relationship, Erich wanted to move quickly: "I just can't help myself, baby, you make me crazy with desire." She relented.

It wasn't long after that when Lin noticed a shift in Erich. He seemed more aloof. His eyes wandered to other women whenever they were out, although he said she was imagining it. At times, he shocked her with cutting "feedback." When she shared her feelings about the changes, Erich scoffed. "A girl like you should be grateful to be with someone like me. You're not all that. I could have anyone I want, you know."

He proved his cruel point soon thereafter, when Lin walked out of class to find Erich parked next to her car, kissing another girl. He glanced up, looked her straight in the eye, smirked, then turned back to the new girl.

If you have lived without consistent patterns of true, unconditional love, it can be difficult to differentiate between love and love-bombing. The former is about you and your happiness, while the latter is about them and their desire to possess, manipulate, and control you. Love-bombing may involve gifts, flattery, excessive compliments, moving too quickly in the beginning of a friendship or romantic relationship, building dependence, and reminders of their "help" and of your past weakness and problems. They promise to fulfill your every dream, but it is all a fantasy. Once you are "won," you are devalued and discarded. You may be criticized, shamed, and compared to others. Romantic partners may cheat and defend their actions by debasing you. Friends may verbally attack.

Conversely, genuine love focuses on your well-being and happiness. The other person desires time together out of appreciation for and enjoyment of who you are. They may compliment you, but it feels natural and genuine, expecting nothing in return. Gifts are never followed by reminders of what they gave or what you owe. If they have helped or "rescued" you in some way, they minimize that action and focus on the present.

The love-bombing gaslighter will study you like a predator does its prey, drawing you in close while hiding behind an elaborate façade of charm. They learn your weaknesses and vulnerabilities, appearing to be a caring listener but intending to use this knowledge to control you. The attachment will seem very real. In close relationships, particularly in sexual relationships, our brains release the hormone *oxytocin*, which fosters loyalty in key relationships. Ideally, this hormone reinforces important social bonds by creating feelings of love and connection. Such feelings, though wonderful to experience, may also override the rational signs of danger.

When the love-bombing gaslighter has lured you in and secured your attachment, the game becomes a bore. At this point, they will begin to devalue you. This isn't actually a shift; this person likely despised or resented you on some level from the beginning, both admiring and feeling threatened by your good qualities. It now becomes their goal to tear down such strengths to restore focus and supremacy to themselves. Here you will see criticism, shaming, minimizing your accomplishments while highlighting their own, speaking derisively about you to others, entitlement, and cashing in on what you "owe" for gifts and favors granted previously.

If you have ever watched a cat with a mouse, you may recognize this pattern. First, the cat studies the rodent with intense interest. Next, the cat toys with its prey, gradually injuring it, releasing it, and attacking again. Eventually, the cat tires of the game and moves on, leaving the mouse either dead or mortally injured; the final outcome matters less than the game. Likewise, the love-bombing gaslighter eventually tires of the sport and moves on to another target. More often than not, the new target is already in their life, in an earlier stage of the game. Such gaslighters, frequently narcissists or sadists, demand constant adoration and will ensure that it is flowing from more than one source.

HOOVERING

Janneke had finally broken away from Mike. She had confronted him with the evidence of his drinking and driving their children while inebriated. With a plan in place and children and packed bags waiting in the car, she finally walked out the door. Years of self-doubt and questioning her sanity as he denied his behavior had held her back from freedom for too long.

Within days, she saw pictures on social media of him with other women, and it stung. But then she got his text message. "Janneke, babe. I lost my job. I can't pay the rent. Could you help me out this once?" Feeling guilty, she transferred him the money. He was the father of her children; she couldn't let him end up on the streets.

The texts and calls increased. Mike came by her apartment with flowers. He pleaded with her to forgive him. He threatened to injure himself if she shut him out. Then one day, he showed up with a car stuffed full, claiming he had lost the apartment. Wouldn't she take him in? It would be like old times. He needed her.

Janneke looked over her shoulder to the faces of her kids, watching. If she said no, she'd be the bad guy. They missed their father. He promised to stop drinking. It would be a new start.

She opened the door wider and let him in.

Hoovering is a common behavioral pattern with gaslighters. After the cycle of love-bombing, devaluing, and discarding, they may move on for a time, filling their vacuous need for adoration elsewhere. But their need to control quickly becomes consuming. The gaslighter sucks you back in with any tactic they can— appeals to shared history, using the kids, promises, pity, or lies. As with a vacuum cleaner, your sense of self and independence is sucked up into the endless void of the gaslighter's need.

Hoovering may take on a familiar shape, re-creating patterns from your early relationship. The love-bombing/devaluation cycle re-emerges and accelerates, not lingering in either stage long enough for you to get comfortable or recognize what they are doing. They may present a combination of apologies, flattery, promises of a better future, and gifts, with a few guilt-trip comments and insults mixed in. You are left feeling unsteady, confused, and insecure, yet hopeful; these feelings are intentionally cultivated to serve the gaslighter's goals. While you might imagine they would dispense with insults at this stage, the rapid injections of criticism serve a calculated purpose: to undermine your confidence so that you are disempowered from leaving.

Watch out for specific acts of gaslighting here. They may spin your shared past with a new slant according to which they are the victim whom you have wronged. If it feels off, trust your gut. The guilt is intentionally engendered. You know what really happened between you, and you know you had good reason to leave. Stay with that.

GHOSTING AND STONEWALLING

Yolanda truly cared about her friend Sandra. They had met in art school and hit it off right away. Sandra quickly suggested that they room together, and Yolanda thought it was a great idea.

At first, living together was great fun. But as Yolanda's social network grew, Sandra seemed to vacillate between affection and fury. When Yolanda went out for sushi with classmates, Sandra stopped speaking to her for a week.

Yolanda asked her repeatedly what was wrong, but Sandra would simply shrug or mutter, "Nothing." After several days, Yolanda sent a heartfelt text message in an attempt to smooth things over. Sandra replied, accusing Yolanda of being "hypersensitive" and "making something out of nothing." She returned to interacting normally but never admitted that anything had been strained. Yolanda felt bewildered. Had she imagined it?

Before long, a wider schism emerged. Yolanda had begun dating someone, and Sandra frequently complained that Yolanda never had time for her anymore. It seemed that whenever Yolanda had a date planned, Sandra had a crisis that she needed to talk through right away.

One night, Yolanda had just left to go dancing with her boyfriend when Sandra texted that she needed to talk. Yolanda decided to ignore the text for a couple of hours, tucking it in the back of her mind to address later.

When she returned to the apartment, Sandra was gone. Yolanda tried responding to her text but received no reply. When she woke the next morning to still no contact, Yolanda began to worry. She found Sandra in class and approached her. Sandra flatly told her she was staying at a friend's place and moved to sit across the room. She ignored Yolanda's texts and attempts to talk for the rest of the week. That weekend, she returned home, packed her things, and left. When Yolanda reached out again to try to understand, she found Sandra had blocked her number.

Sandra demonstrates many characteristics of gaslighters, beginning with the cycle of love-bombing, devaluing, and discarding. She then engages in stonewalling, cutting off contact or giving Yolanda the silent treatment in a controlling bid to place her roommate in the position of pursuing her. Finally, Sandra ghosts Yolanda by moving out and blocking her number without ever attempting to resolve the conflict.

Gaslighters use these maneuvers to control the relationship dynamics and those within their sphere of influence. They tug at your heartstrings and compel concern, manipulating you to worry that you may have done something to hurt their feelings as they silently withdraw. This places you in the position of pursuing reconciliation and allows them to retain power and moral superiority.

ENABLERS

Gaslighters frequently surround themselves with enablers to support their nefarious agendas. Colloquially called flying monkeys after the Wicked Witch's minions in *The Wizard of Oz*, they help gaslighters carry out their selfish goals in a form of abuse by proxy.

Flying monkeys don't necessarily recognize their role; they may be innocent actors who have themselves been manipulated into believing in the fabricated reality. They might genuinely believe they are supporting a just cause and may have been charmed into believing that the gaslighter is good.

Alternatively, more perceptive enablers may be seeking celebrity by association and thus willing to do the dirty work to curry favor with a popular or powerful gaslighter. Politicians in the authoritarian's political party, believing in the party's cornerstone values, may become flying monkeys as they justify and cover up for extreme behaviors.

Enablers often play out a common family pattern of scapegoating one individual, a situation known in family therapy as creating an "identified patient." They side with the gaslighter in victim-blaming and shaming. For example, family members too often slut-shame the molestation survivor who tells of their abuse and accuse them of ruining the abusive family member's life through their brave disclosure. Pastoral counselors may emphasize fidelity and forgiveness in the face of abuse in a marriage or take a "both sides are wrong" position, which excuses the abuser from their responsibility to protect the other. Spouses engage in enabling when they justify abuse of the children as "discipline" and shift focus to the child's misbehavior.

Flying monkey behaviors may involve spying, gossiping, threatening, reinforcing the narrative that the gaslighter is the true victim, and concealing misdeeds. Gaslighters enlist such support using charm and charisma, directly or indirectly promising rewards, esteem, and high positions. In shaping the narrative about their target through derisive speech, they assuage misgivings and reinforce the idea that they are right to act as they do.

WHAT YOU'VE BEEN TAUGHT ABOUT BOUNDARIES

Innate to gaslighting is a lack of respect for you as an individual. It's no surprise, then, that gaslighters constantly encroach on others' boundaries. This erodes these healthy frameworks and empowers the gaslighter to exert their will in the relationship.

Recognizing such boundary crossing as it happens can be difficult. Erosion is a slow and gradual process. Sometimes It can even feel like love, because they are always there, constantly showing interest or concern. They may excuse intrusions with statements such as "I just miss you so much" or "I'm only jealous because you mean so much to me."

To complicate matters, if you grew up in an enmeshed parent-child relationship where your autonomy wasn't respected, the hovering, checking, rigid rules, withholding or other punish-ments, and boundary-crossing of a gaslighter in adulthood may feel normal or expected, whether this is the same parent or a new relationship. Without experience in a healthy relationship, it can be hard to know what respect feels like. With such conditioning, what sets off warning signals to one person may strike you as benign or even normal.

A Healthy Approach toward Relationships

It is important to have a vision of what a healthy relation-ship looks like. This contrast helps you evaluate your present patterns and provides a vision for the future. In a healthy relationship, you are able to take up space. You can set limits, say no, or choose what to give of yourself, and those around you accept and respect such boundaries with grace. In turn, you allow others to express their needs and wants and show consideration of them without feeling responsible for fulfilling or fixing them. There is a sense of respect, mutuality, and elevation of one another.

YOU FEEL OBLIGATED TO RELATIONSHIPS AND OTHER PEOPLE

If you grew up in an emotionally abusive environment, you may have taken the role of pacifier. While some children push back against toxicity and often receive even worse treatment as a result, other children observe the pattern and take a survival approach of becoming the good or perfect child. This is an enor-mous emotional burden to shoulder, because these children take on the responsibility of regulating or soothing the behavior of the adults in their lives, who ought to be doing so for them.

In following this pattern throughout your developmental years and receiving the reinforcement of attention and even favoritism—or at the very least fewer parental attacks—your brain develops reward circuitry that reinforces pleasing others. It becomes neurologically hardwired that to please, or to "fawn," equates to safety and survival, whether literal or emotional.

It should be of little surprise, then, that this pattern isn't easily broken. As you develop outside relationships, whether as a child with teachers and friends, or as an adult with romantic partners, bosses, or spiritual communities, deferring to authoritarian personalities may feel natural, appropriate, and even safe. It becomes difficult or seemingly impossible to say no to others, as an internalized developmental trauma reaction subconsciously signals that saying no is dangerous, while going along is what good people do. This pattern of experience shaped Kendra's dating life.

When Kendra was hired, her manager Arman seemed to take an immediate liking to her. She noticed that she was always scheduled to work under Arman, and he often called her in for extra shifts. Kendra quickly responded, afraid to displease him by saying no.

One day, Kendra found herself alone in the break room with Arman. He took her by the shoulders and forcefully kissed her. She pulled away in shock, and he smiled at her (or was it a leer?), then left the room. Later that evening, Kendra received a text message from Arman: "I'm taking you to the movies after work tomorrow. Bring something cute to change into." Uncomfortable but unsure how to respond, Kendra simply wrote back, "Okay."

In this story, Kendra demonstrates the fawn reaction, in which a survivor of developmental abuse learns to diffuse conflict to create a sense of normalcy and safety in the face of what most people might react to as potential danger or boundary intrusions. Subconsciously, repeated parental messages of *"Don't you say no to me, young lady!"* and *"You do NOT walk away from me!"* shaped her ongoing inability to assert herself.

People subjected to childhood emotional abuse and punished for expressing needs may develop a fawning response that follows them through life. You learn that to coexist or meet crucial attachment needs you must become servile and useful, surrendering any needs that might inconvenience the other. This creates a codependence, the cornerstone of which is the inability to express rights, wants, and needs. You may surrender quickly if conflict arises and stay in unhealthy relationships hoping for scraps of attention, kindness, or praise.

It is not difficult to see how such conditioning prepares you to be targeted by gaslighters, who keenly perceive these unfulfilled attachment needs and fawning patterns and manipulate them to their personal benefit. When you have been shown in childhood that relationships do not involve equality, you're predisposed to accept this pattern throughout life.

Know that such teaching is a lie. You do not have to be in a relationship with someone, or submit to them, because it is what they want. You are exceedingly precious and valuable whether in relationships or on your own. You deserve relationships with people who see your value, love you for it, and do not regard you as an object to possess. You deserve to be honored, cherished, and respected as an equal in every relationship.

YOU FEAR ANGER AND REJECTION

Fear is a powerful motivator, whether toward action or stillness. Fear triggers your innate fight-or-flight response, activated by the amygdala deep in the core of your brain. This activation floods your nervous system with hormones to prepare you for survival through fighting, fleeing from danger, or freezing like an animal playing dead. This is a rapid, subconscious response. It is innate and instinctual; these reactions are nothing to be ashamed of.

Gaslighters tap into your natural fear responses by unleashing anger, associated with physical danger, or implicitly threatening rejection, activating your instinctual sense that your survival is threatened by isolation. As a species, we are biologically pro-grammed to react strongly to either scenario.

Your personal trauma history will shape this innate neural wiring. If you grew up in an environment infused with angry outbursts, whether toward you, between your parents, or in your community, your fear response pattern becomes supercharged and primed to reactivity. Likewise, if you grew up with neglect or rejection at home or school, your sensitivity to signs of rejection will be heightened. Making sense of your history is key to understanding how you respond to the gaslighter in your life today.

Sadistic gaslighters cunningly identify and exploit your sensitivities. Rather than using such perception to envelop you with reassurance, protection, or love, they use these wounds to manipulate you in their callous games. They lash out strategically to coerce compliance, then pivot to kindness before your pain has time to harden into resolve, keeping you within their snare.

This pattern challenges your ability to set and enforce boundaries and dampens any efforts to stand up for yourself. Understanding the source of your fear and your fight-flight-freeze response creates room for self-compassion. This can provide a measure of freedom from the cycle. It is normal to feel bad when others express anger toward you. Notice your feelings, breathe through them, and give yourself grace.

You have the right to your boundaries, no matter how scary it feels.

THE MORE YOU KNOW

Having accepted that you have endured gaslighting, you may feel a growing spark of empowerment in building your understanding of these cycles and their effects on your life. Understanding how your life experiences may have created vulnerability to gaslighting illuminates areas that could benefit from deeper healing. Hold that awareness with self-compassion; we will discuss the healing process in more depth in the sections ahead.

This is not a place for self-judgment. Allow no room for self-critical thoughts like "How could I have not seen this sooner?" It is impossible to view a whole ship from an interior cabin. Consider this a map that provides a layout of the ship. You choose whether to use this map to guide you to the outside and decide whether or not to disembark.

The following exercises are designed to help you recognize and begin to disentangle from the cycles discussed here. Keep your journal nearby as you mindfully move through following the prompts.

EXERCISE 1: IDENTIFYING PATTERNS

As you read step 2, what cycles or patterns stood out to you? With what did you most identify? Take a moment to name the cycle that felt most familiar to you, and list examples from your own relationship that followed this pattern. As you write, notice what feelings are activated and where you hold tension in your body. Listen to what it tells you and note that, too.

Cycle or pattern:_____

_____

Examples from my life:_____

_____

_____

_____

_____

_____

_____

_____

_____

EXERCISE 2: ADDRESSING FEAR OF ANGER

Working from the simple truth that where we look impacts how we feel, this exercise incorporates gazespotting and mindfulness principles from Brainspotting therapy with guided visualization to reduce maladaptive fear reactions.

Picture a recent moderately distressing verbal conflict. Notice your instinct to run away, to defend or counterattack, or the way you feel stuck when conflict arises. Remind yourself that these reactions are natural.

Breathe deeply and slowly, to counteract the shallow breathing that accompanies fear. This helps restore blood flow to your brain, allowing you to access your higher-order decision-making capacities. Even before it feels natural, shift your body posture to one of confidence, opening your chest and lifting your chin, and notice the emotional shift that accompanies this movement.

Envision standing up for yourself and speaking assertively in this scenario that sparks fear of rejection or wrath. How does it make you feel? Where in your body can you access a reservoir of strength or calm? Hold this dual awareness together.

Notice where your eyes naturally go as you picture this, and allow your gaze to rest on an object in that region. You can stay there and notice what comes up in images or in bodily sensations, or mindfully explore your visual field from left to right, stopping at any point where you feel that bodily reservoir of strength most strongly. Find a fixed point in this region, either near or far from you, and let your gaze rest there, just noticing what happens internally. Take your time here.

When you are ready, perhaps feeling a greater sense of peace, calm, or courage, close your eyes for a moment and take a deep, slow breath. Note any new insights in your journal.

EXERCISE 3: EXPLORING OBLIGATION

List three times you have done something because you felt you couldn't say no.

1. _____

   _____

2. _____

   _____

3. _____

   _____

How did each situation turn out? What feelings do you have about each scenario as you look back on it? Take a moment to envision a positive outcome that follows setting a limit in each of these three scenarios.

After reading this chapter, you're now equipped with acceptance that what has been happening is real and a greater understanding of the patterns and cycles that maintained this abusive relationship. Now it's time to release some of the emotions that this growing awareness has unearthed. In step 3, we will explore why grief is a necessary and healing process.

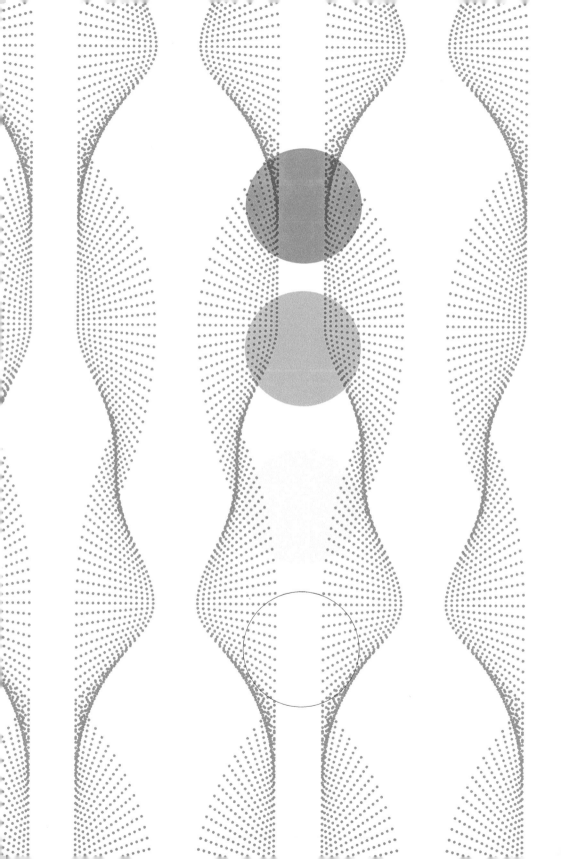

STEP 3:
LET
YOURSELF
GRIEVE

As the truth and weight of all you have suffered becomes apparent, it can be tempting to retreat to patterns of avoidance, depression, or denial. Grief is something different. Though painful, this step will help you release some of that hurt and move through it. Please be gentle with yourself as you work through this chapter.

WHY GRIEF?

Accepting that you have been experiencing a pattern of gaslighting, manipulation, and emotional abuse, and that such patterns are entrenched and unlikely to change, brings with it a certain loss. There is a loss of hope that this relationship might be or become something that it is not, and perhaps the loss of a fantasy fairy-tale ending. For those who choose to cut ties with the gaslighter, there is loss of the relationship itself, which, albeit unhealthy, provided a much-needed human connection. And with that, there is painful awareness of time lost.

Just as attachment at the beginning of any relationship is gradual, so is the process of letting go. Feelings build in significance and intensity and likewise take time to recede and resolve. Because close relationships are so significant to what it means to be human, it is impossible to escape the grief that results when relationships fail to live up to our needs, hopes, and expectations.

If you don't move through the healing pain of grief, you may lose parts of yourself and the opportunity to make sense of your life story by simply cutting off that difficult period of your past. You also lose the opportunity to understand yourself fully in the present. You continue to carry the pain of what you have lost through this relationship, while forfeiting the diamonds of good created under such pressure—the personal growth that comes from reflection, acceptance, and the closure of grief.

Without a grief process, you may continue to feel the pain on a dull level over many years, remaining in the initial stage of numbness and denial. Such unresolved grief is likely to express itself for years through depression, low self-esteem, physical ailments, and negative impacts on other relationships. It becomes more difficult to let go and move forward.

As painful as it is, we can never skip the grief process. Loss weighs us down until it is faced and released. What you are feeling is real. Allow yourself the release of grief.

EXPERIENCING A LOSS

When you accept the reality that you are in a relationship with a gaslighter, you may experience a profound sense of loss. This loss is genuine, though outwardly different from the loss of a relationship to death. Such disenfranchised grief may not be recognized by others and lacks the typical rituals and comforts of mourning, yet it represents a significant loss and shift in your inner world and its outward organization.

Grief can look very different, reflecting the uniqueness of each individual and the loss you are mourning. Many themes, or stages, are common to grief. These stages tend to follow a general order, but it is common to revisit earlier phases as you work toward resolving a loss.

You may have gone through a period of *denial* at some time prior to or while beginning this book. You may even vacillate in periods of denial and numbness now. That's okay; just name and recognize it for what it is. It's all part of the process.

Cascades of immense pain frequently follow as denial gives way to clarity. You may experience guilt or self-blame over aspects of the relationship. This can be an emotionally flooding, overwhelming stage.

Anger often comes next, dulling the pain by hardening it into something that feels more powerful. In the unique grief of a relationship with a gaslighter, there is a particular validity to your anger. Allow yourself to feel this. Listen to what it has to tell you. Don't be afraid of your fire. Let it burn. It may flare high, but it will burn lower, too, to gently glowing embers.

Bargaining is a common element of grief. In mourning the loss of an unhealthy relationship, bargaining can mean repeated attempts to reunify, reasoning that "if only" you do something different, perhaps you can change the outcome. Bargaining comes from the desperation of pain and the ghosts of lingering denial.

Depression eventually follows as reality sets in. This may involve a period of reflection. It can also be lonely, particularly when your gaslighter has cut you off from having other significant relationships in your life.

Through this process of reflection, *acceptance* grows and strengthens, bringing with it a sense of calm and of hope. You are able to reimagine life without this noxious relationship. New possibilities emerge.

COMPLEX GRIEF

It had been 11 months since Jordan left Marc. So why was it still so difficult to move forward? She rarely left her room, showered infrequently, seldom slept, and vacillated between rage and a depression so low that she found herself imagining ways to end her life.

Jordan had finally awakened to the truth that Marc was not good for her. He would take her on trips and bring her flowers, then turn around and berate her in front of their friends. On several occasions, he struck her, but he reassured her that this happened with every couple, and it wasn't like it happened every day. When she tried to address the problems, Marc denied his past actions. Jordan felt helpless and angry, but Marc dismissed her as hysterical. She internalized this blame, and the patterns continued.

When she finally identified the pattern as abuse, Jordan moved home with her mother. Her mom told her that she was too old to find a man now, and that she should have settled for Marc. Jordan took to watching hours of TV and endlessly scrolling social media to drown out the painful thoughts.

It was hard not to miss Marc. When she scrolled through old photos of them together, his good looks still took her breath away. Seeing current images of him on social media with new girls crushed and enraged Jordan. She missed being desired and felt worthless being alone. She questioned whether it had been so bad, or whether perhaps she could have fixed things if only she hadn't become so upset so often.

Jordan displays a complicated grief reaction. The loss of her relationship may be considered a *disenfranchised grief,* because it lacks the typical mourning rituals that facilitate processing loss. Disenfranchisement increases the likelihood that such grief may devolve into a complex reaction. If you were dependent upon the person you lost, a pattern fostered by gaslighters, you will be more prone to suffer a complex or complicated grief. If you have had a long-term relationship with a gaslighter, such as with a parent, it's more likely that the grief you experience will be complex.

Complicated grief is marked by an extended period beyond six months when you continue to feel unbearable pain. You may experience an inability to sleep, anger, or loss of basic self-care and give up on socializing or participating in hobbies or activities. You may find yourself lost in continual fantasies about the gaslighter, yearning to reunite. This may be accompanied by intense feelings of loneliness and emptiness, which may be heightened if your gaslighter isolated you.

At their worst, complex grief reactions can lead to suicidal ideation or attempts. If you find yourself contemplating such thoughts, reach out for help from a mental health therapist or a local crisis hotline (see the Resources section on page 149 for options). Things may feel hopeless right now, but these feelings will change as you move through the grief. Hold on.

You may question why you would feel such strong feelings toward someone who has been so hurtful. Relationships are nuanced, and our need for attachment adapts even in adverse circumstances. You may be someone with a big, compassionate heart who sees the good in broken people. That's a wonderful quality, but it shouldn't come at the cost of abandoning all boundaries. You can validate others' humanity or even love them without laying yourself down to be abused.

This natural propensity to bond can lead people to develop strong feelings of affection and loyalty even in extreme circumstances. Stockholm syndrome describes situations in which people form attachments to their aggressor and distrust potential helpers. In the Swedish bank robbery scenario for which it was named, captives went so far as to rationalize being shot in the leg, a nonlethal wound, as a sign of the robber's goodwill. One hostage went on to marry her captor years later, after he finished his prison sentence. Perhaps you can relate to rationalizing abuses because they were interspersed with moments of affection.

Coming to grips with a Stockholm syndrome reaction can cause an added layer of complicated grief. To realize that what you had was not real can bring feelings of shame, humiliation, and sorrow. Be gentle with yourself as you navigate this layered, complex grief.

GRIEVING THE TIME YOU LOST

Disenfranchised grief differs from bereavement in that when the grief is over a broken relationship, there is an added layer of loss of time invested. You may mourn lost opportunities to explore other, healthier relationships. You may look back on the years spent trying to be the perfect child, romantic partner, employee, or friend, only to have it implode. Perhaps you deferred personal goals or gave up on significant dreams. You may have endured isolation and missed out on opportunities to develop supportive friendships.

You may be facing, for the first time, the reality that you never had an adequately supportive parent-child relationship. This can usher in grief over who you might have been, had you been shaped in a more encouraging environment. You may feel sorrow for how long you've allowed yourself to listen to lies and believe the worst about yourself. Allow yourself to feel that sorrow, and let it propel you toward a kinder self-love.

What you have lost is real. Your feelings have merit, but you can mourn these losses and emerge from them to a brighter future, making the most of the time ahead. Allow yourself this time to grieve.

FORGIVE YOURSELF

It may be tempting to berate yourself for staying in a relationship with this toxic person or becoming entangled with them in the first place. Please don't beat yourself up. You've received enough of that already. In fact, the emotional abuse you've endured may be where your inner voice learned its harsh, critical tone.

Part of finding freedom from gaslighting relationships is evicting them from your mental space. Do not allow them to take up residence in your mind by shaping your self-talk. You deserve only kindness and compassion.

You are not to blame. No matter what you've overlooked, accepted, forgiven, or failed to see, no matter what faults you brought to the relationship or how much you did or did not fight back, gaslighting is never your fault. The blame for lies and manipulation falls solely on the shoulders of the one who treated you as something to control and maneuver rather than a soul to cherish and protect.

Your only responsibilities are to come to terms with what is and what has happened, to grieve and release what was and what was not, and to make self-caring choices moving forward.

FEEL YOUR FEELINGS

Whatever you are feeling, know that it is valid and you are allowed to feel it. Observe your feelings with compassion and give yourself grace. There's no right way to feel about your uniquely difficult relationship.

Your emotions may seem all over the place. One day you may feel angry, and the next you may be aching with sadness. You may find yourself feeling wistful or hollow with loneliness or regret. You may have times of feeling hopeful, and then find yourself triggered into rage again.

This isn't a setback. It is all part of the healing process, as new layers are peeled away and raw spots revealed. Notice the triggers. Write them down. Sit with the source of the anger until it melts into something softer. Find the pain and allow yourself to grieve that. Whatever it is, you must feel it to heal it.

It can be helpful to talk to someone you trust, such as a therapist or a friend. Let them know that you just need someone to listen without offering judgment or suggestions. It can be healing to experience that you aren't isolated in your hurt, nor do you have to bear it alone.

And when you have sat with the painful feelings for a while, get up. Turn on some music that will set a mood you want to embrace. Move to a different room or, preferably, go outdoors. As you shift your view, you can more easily leave behind those thoughts associated with where you processed them. As you engage in something active or creative, whether jogging, baking, cleaning, painting, or fixing something broken, you will find a shift in energy and mood. As you take action, you may notice that the pain is not static. It can change, and so can you.

Affirmations for Grief

As you mourn your losses, repeating affirmations and mantras can help create positive, healing neuropathways in your brain. This reinforces comforting truths and makes space to move gently through grief to resolution. Sit with each of these and see what resonates, or write down a few of your own.

- I embrace healing.
- My broken heart will again be whole.
- I allow myself to fully feel this pain.
- I accept this loss and release resistance.
- My grief will not last forever.
- I release the hurt and carry the good forward.
- The universe is full of love, and I am part of it.
- I am not alone.
- _____
- _____
- _____

MOVING THROUGH GRIEF

It had been a month since Ray left her faith community. She could no longer internalize the accusations of faithlessness whenever she asked questions about their beliefs. She had observed—and heard denials of—too many contradictions between their scriptural values and their actions. When the leader slid a hand onto her bottom during a hug, she was appalled. But it was the hateful accusations of making it up to hurt the leader that crushed her.

Ray was heartbroken and felt utterly alone. Even the few friends who remained loyal seemed to dismiss her pain with spiritual platitudes. She mourned the loss of her community and the surety of her faith. She was ashamed that she had spent so long accepting such gaslighting as normal when she saw it happen to others. Ray allowed herself to feel her sorrow. She journaled about her loss, anger, and loneliness, and she prayed.

As she allowed herself to feel her whole range of emotions, Ray noticed that the deep lows came less frequently. She wasn't sure yet how she felt about trying again with a new faith community, but the idea didn't repulse her anymore, either. For the first time in many weeks, Ray felt a sense of hope.

The grief process is as unique as the individual and the loss suffered. If you left a toxic relationship with a partner, your grief may involve a lot of life reorganization. Grieving the loss of the supportive mother you never had or the secure childhood you were not afforded may be a more private, hidden pain, yet profound. Perhaps your grief encompasses a job that ended as you began to stand up against workplace gaslighting, leaving you to face not only uncertainty but loss of years invested. These various scenarios all carry their own grief patterns.

What unites them is the necessity of allowing yourself to feel the pain, to courageously and compassionately journey through it. Grief subsides as we face the losses but holds us captive when we try to ignore it. There is no right way to feel and no perfect path through this messy stage. The only constant is the need for awareness and grace.

As in Ray's example, when grief begins to abate, hope arises with gentle presence. You may emerge with a new sense of meaning or understanding about yourself, others, and the world, a hard-won wisdom. You may discover a quiet energy that infuses you with the will to move forward. Right now, these things may feel impossibly far off, and that's okay. Just notice where you are right now and don't rush. You will get there.

Grief can feel like being adrift, unmoored, and directionless—scary feelings when you are in the middle of an uncomfortable or painful stage. While there is no road map to guide you through the uniqueness of your pain, the following exercises may help facilitate your process.

EXERCISE 1: WRITE A LETTER

Grief is often accompanied by feelings of incompletion. There is always more you want to say but cannot, either because you can no longer reach the person you want to say it to or because it would be unwise. To help resolve the multilayered emotions of your grief, consider writing a letter. This letter could be directed to the gaslighter, to the flying monkeys, or even to yourself. Allow yourself unfettered expression of your shock, anger, desire to bargain, sadness, and perhaps acceptance.

You may wish to write a series of letters, or a singular letter symbolically saying goodbye. The purpose of such writing is not to get in one last communication but to grant yourself space to express what is left unsaid. These letters can then be tucked away in a journal, shredded, or safely burned in a final act of closure.

EXERCISE 2: MAKING ADJUSTMENTS

Grief is always accompanied by patterns of readjustment, whether large or small. To help you through this reorganization stage, take your journal and spend some time writing freely in response to the following prompts:

- Internal adjustments: Who am I now, as I recognize the gaslighting for what it is?
- External adjustments: What changes do I want to make as I grieve what this relationship lacks?
- Spiritual adjustments: How has this experience impacted my beliefs and understanding of myself, others, and the world? What meaning can I find in this?

EXERCISE 3: LIGHT STREAM MEDITATION FOR GRIEF

This meditation adapts the light stream resource from eye movement desensitization and reprocessing (EMDR) therapy to assist with moving through grief associated with gaslighting.

Find a comfortable place to sit or lie down. Close your eyes and let your attention shift to your breath. Notice the rise and fall of your chest and the rhythm of your breath slowing down. Breathe in slowly, filling your lungs, and gently release your breath.

When you're ready, allow yourself to bring an image of the gaslighter to mind. Notice what feelings arise and accept them without judgment. Scan your body and observe where you hold tension. Where do the feelings reside? Let your attention rest there as you continue breathing, slowly, deeply, with intention.

Picture a glowing orb of light swirling above the crown of your head in a warm, comforting color. Watch it begin to flow down into the crown of your head. Let it flow down your arms and into your fingertips. Observe the light gently wrap its warmth around any hard, tense places in your body where the grief or anger is held. Watch as the hard edges soften and the tension loosens. Don't rush; stay with it and just observe with compassion as your emotions feel as they do. Notice as the tension gently subsides.

Observe yourself, still here, still breathing. Notice the strength you hold to endure this pain. Recognize your courage to face this grief. Notice your breath, the steady rise and fall of your chest. Still here. Soft, yet strong. Still breathing.

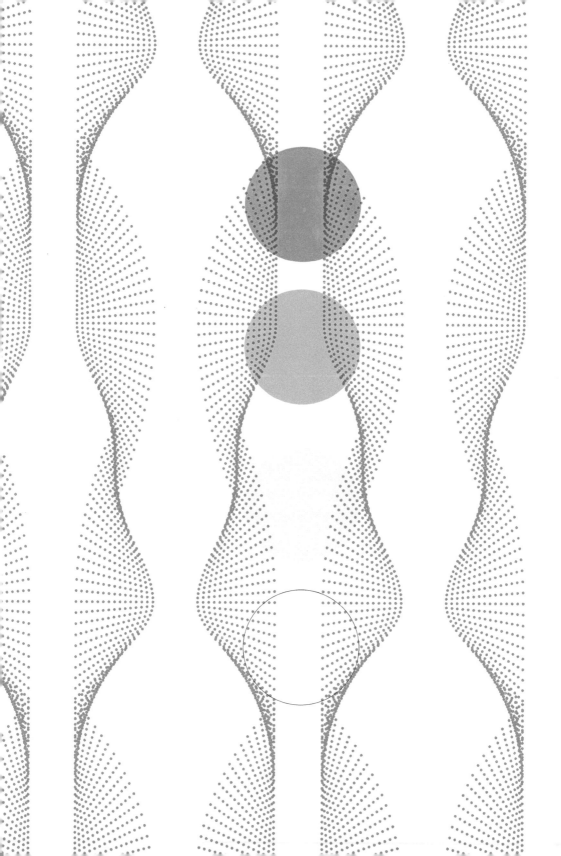

STEP 4:
FOCUS ON YOURSELF

As you move through grief, a process of turning inward begins. This is not selfishness; rather, it is an intentional phase to heal what has been neglected for too long. You matter, and your mental well-being matters. Allow yourself the grace of this essential step toward healing.

HEALING FROM EMOTIONAL ABUSE

Emotional abuse takes its toll on you gradually, in a compounding escalation of wounds. Gaslighters chip away at your sense of sanity incrementally, slowly ungrounding you with each assault on your rational foundation. It is only natural, then, that healing likewise comes gradually. It is important to be patient with yourself. Don't try to rush the process or criticize yourself when it doesn't happen overnight. Give yourself time to heal.

To release the wounds you have internalized, you must first face them. This can be painful, but you have to feel it to heal it. Just as a surgeon opens up the body to remove a tumor, the source of your emotional pain must be revealed to allow deep healing to begin.

As a patient recovers from a medical intervention, they must change their typical patterns and "take it easy" for a little while. They may need to relearn how to use an injured part, decrease activity, get more rest, and allow others to help care for them for a while. Recovery takes priority for a period, but regular patterns eventually resume. Emotional healing follows a similar process.

As you move through grief toward healing, you begin to come back to yourself. Who were you before this relationship shrank you down? Who might you be if not inhibited by constant criticism and confusion? What have you given up or lost that you might like to reclaim?

For some, it might be hard to identify a "before." Perhaps the emotional abuse has been there as long as you can remember. This may require a more imaginative process, if there is no conscious sense of self to return to. The wounded child inside you may need compassion and love to allow them to grow into the potential that has been dormant for so long.

MOVING THROUGH THE HEALING PROCESS

Take a moment to pause and take stock of where you are right now. Recognize how far you have already come. Celebrate that, even as you continue to press onward and inward.

As you move through the healing process, be gentle with yourself, and practice self-care that honors your spirit. It is okay to let go of some things in your life, to say no to new projects and commitments, so that you can preserve your energy and focus on this essential work. Make time for introspection, perhaps even scheduling time on your calendar for inner work.

Consider who might support you through this step. Do you have trusted friends or loved ones who are capable of holding space for you, of listening without gaslighting, dismissing, lecturing, or rushing to solutions? This might be difficult if your world has narrowed and your trust in others has eroded from constant exposure to gaslighting. A therapist can be an irreplaceable ally and safe sounding board to help you process and release the wounds of emotional abuse while providing a reparative experience of an emotionally healthy relationship.

EMBRACE SELF-COMPASSION

I'm such an idiot, Corwin thought, hurrying back to his car. The dirty look he had just received from the barista he'd tried to compliment still burned in his mind. No wonder I'm alone. He caught his reflection in the window, scowling back at himself, and paused.

No, Corwin corrected himself. I'm human; I make mistakes. Maybe it's not even about me. He took a steadying breath and got in the car. That kind of criticism sounded like his controlling older brother. He was done letting him rule his life. Corwin turned on his favorite music and rolled down the windows, savoring the cool breeze, leaving the moment behind.

Self-compassion is essential to emotional healing and growth. Recognizing gaslighting and the pain it's caused leaves you at a crossroads: to internalize and continue that hurt through self-criticism or to be tender and kind toward yourself. Many people don't recognize that this is a choice. Self-compassion is an option.

You may have been taught that criticism makes you a better person. Gaslighters may use this excuse to justify their cruelty. In truth, harsh criticism merely handicaps. The alternative is not to deny faults or failings but to accept your own fallibility with tenderness. Try to develop tolerance for imperfection. This doesn't mean giving up on doing your best but reflects a radical acceptance of yourself without conditions.

If this is hard to imagine, try this thought exercise: Picture yourself as a three-year-old child. Imagine that you have just created a messy, colorful, joyful finger-painted work of art. You show it proudly to your preschool teacher or parent. What response does that three-year-old you want and need? If you could travel back in time to receive that painting from your younger self, how would you respond?

I imagine it would be a response of warmth, appreciation, and compassion, with awareness that Little You did their best. You would probably see the beautiful humanity in that uninhibited creative act and embrace your younger self. This is the spirit of self-compassion. You do not demand or expect perfection. You give grace for mistakes, and you anticipate growth without rushing it.

As you allow yourself to heal from the gaslighting and emotional abuse you have suffered, be patient, gentle, and kind with yourself. Forgive yourself for the past and for mistakes you make in the present. Accept that you aren't and won't be perfect, but that if you do your best, your best is good enough. You are unconditionally worthy.

Self-Talk

Negative self-talk is the nemesis of self-compassion. Unfortunately, it is so easy to fall into, particularly if it's been modeled and trained into your psyche. To undo these patterns of negativity, it is crucial to create new mental patterns by intentionally speaking gracious words to yourself where self-criticism comes so readily.

- **Instead of** *"I'm such a screw-up; I never do anything right,"* **try** *"I make mistakes. I will try again. I am learning and growing."*
- **Instead of** *"No one loves me,"* **try** *"I don't have to be everyone's cup of tea. I accept myself for who I am. I am loveable and worthy."*

Remember that what we rehearse is what we reinforce. It is time to leave self-criticism behind.

WORK TOWARD RESOLVING PAST WOUNDS

Leticia knew the abuse wasn't her fault, but she continued to feel shame and guilt. Then a friend suggested that she try eye movement desensitization and reprocessing (EMDR) therapy.

In EMDR, Leticia shared her feelings of shame and belief that "It's all my fault," noticing how she felt like curling into a little ball as she spoke. As the therapist guided Leticia in tracking her eyes back and forth to stimulate both brain hemispheres, Leticia experienced a rush of related memories moving through her mind, connecting this guilty feeling to multiple incidents with her abuser as well as in childhood. As Leticia followed the threads of memory, sharing observations between sets of eye movements, she felt her emotions swell and subside. The knot in her stomach loosened, and she found herself sitting up straighter. By the session's end she was exhausted, much like after a long cry.

Leticia slept hard that night, her dreams filled with memories of her abuser, but this time she dreamed of standing up to him. When she returned to therapy the following week, she noted that her self-blaming thoughts had disappeared. She was ready to tackle something new.

When you have experienced gaslighting and abuse, particularly when it has persisted over time, it can be invaluable to seek out the support of a competent therapist who specializes in treating trauma within relationships. Therapy provides a safe, containing environment in which not only to unpack the painful stories you carry but to experience a reparative relationship with someone who will lovingly hold space for you, supporting you without judgment. Dr. David Grand, the founder of Brainspotting therapy, refers to this as *dual attunement*—the way therapists focus on the neurological processes of healing while simultaneously being attuned to the verbal and nonverbal communication and dynamics between you, forming a holding container for distress.

Brainspotting is another powerful therapy that you might consider to help you through this inward-focused step of healing. Brainspotting harnesses the power of focused mindfulness with awareness of where you hold the emotional distress in your body, while identifying a fixed visual spot to gaze at as you process and release the emotional pain of the past. The visual spot is carefully selected to access the neurological network where the targeted memories are stored, thereby fully activating and releasing their power. Rather than side-to-side eye movements, as with EMDR, Brainspotting typically uses bilateral music—music specially designed to move from one ear to the other—to enhance reprocessing of painful memories. All this is anchored within the safety and emotional support of a caring therapist who journeys with you as you focus inward.

Both EMDR and Brainspotting harness the brain's innate neuroplasticity, or ability to change itself, to heal at a deeper level by processing distressing memories. By simultaneously activating the parts of the brain that store the memory and related feelings, these approaches create deep, lasting changes. You release the impacts of damaging memories from where they are stored in the brain and body, rather than simply trying to think differently about them. When memory is adaptively resolved, symptoms of trauma such as nightmares, flashbacks, and intrusive memories recede.

Where trauma results from interpersonal pain, interpersonal processes are necessary to deeply heal. The support of a skilled, empathic therapist is invaluable in your healing journey.

REMEMBER, YOU CAN'T "FIX" AN ABUSER

As you focus on yourself and your own healing, it can be tempting to think, *Why isn't the gaslighter the one in therapy?* You might revert to the bargaining stage of grief and start to imagine an alternate reality in which they also do this inner work, come to new insights, and become a changed person. You may be tempted to share your new insights with the gaslighter in hopes of changing them and creating the happy home, friendship, or workplace you desire. Perhaps if you just explain to them how they are gaslighting you, they'll change.

But you can't fix an abuser. You can only allow yourself to heal. People *can* change—even abusers—but no one changes who doesn't intrinsically desire it. Sadistic and narcissistic gaslighters lack the courageous vulnerability necessary for growth.

What you can and must do is focus on yourself and foster your own healing. You deserve to be free from the wounds and scars they have inflicted. If you remain in a relationship with them, trust that your own growth will change something in the dynamic, but keep your own health as your motivation.

GET IN TOUCH WITH YOUR OWN NEEDS AND PREFERENCES

After a long period of external control, you may have lost touch with your sense of self, including your own preferences, wants, and needs. Your needs have been shamed, ignored, scorned, and trampled upon by the gaslighter, but they never went away.

There is nothing wrong with your needs or desires. They are part of what makes you human and your exquisite self! Give yourself permission to identify and own your needs.

Becoming aware of your body sense is a good place to start if you feel out of touch with yourself. Close your eyes and slowly scan your body from head to toe. Notice any sensation, tension, or tightness. Wherever you find sensation, pause and hold your attention there. Stay with the feeling and explore what it may be telling you. There may be immediate and deeper meanings that become apparent. Your tensed shoulders may suggest the need to drop them back, straighten your posture, or move your neck. They may also be signaling anxiety or defensiveness. If you sense such a connection, stay with it and see where it leads. As you scan your body, you might feel nothing. That's okay, too; just notice the nothingness with gentle, open curiosity.

Whatever your needs may be, stay open to them with warm interest. Needs are not wrong. There is no shame. You deserve to seek their fulfillment and to extend compassion inward when need fulfillment is deferred.

You also get to enjoy preferences. If you have been controlled for a long time, you may not have ventured into trying new things, or you may have been discouraged from interests that were true to you. Now is a time to explore these possibilities. Try new foods, take that belly-dance class, grow that beard, wear the combat boots or the miniskirt, or both! Cast aside the rulebook and figure out what makes you feel like *you*.

As you let go of having to please the gaslighter in your life and find freedom from the confusion they triggered, you begin to cultivate space for *you*. When you know, respect, and love yourself, you can show up wholeheartedly and confidently in relationships.

This may mean standing solidly against waves that attempt to knock you back down or finding the courage to choose when and from whom to walk away. Instead of choosing to appease the gaslighter or make them happy, you choose you.

PRACTICE SELF-LOVE

If you've spent a great deal of time with a narcissistic gaslighter in your life, the concept of self-love may make you cringe. It's important to distinguish between the insecure, self-promoting, attention-seeking self-absorption of narcissism and the centered, often quiet confidence of self-love. This isn't a question of extroversion versus introversion but of confidence and compassion.

Narcissism says, *I matter most,* while self-love says, *I matter, too.* From a place of security grounded in your value, you are empowered to love others even more fully than before. You may well discover that love has a limitless magic to it, destroying the narcissist's myth that to value others is to become less.

Self-love grows from a deep compassion for yourself. You don't pretend to be flawless or infallible, but you radically accept yourself as a complex and radiant mosaic of broken and beautiful pieces. You extend inward the grace that you might naturally extend outward. When you mess up, you forgive yourself. You excuse the harsh inner critic and replace it with a voice of warmth. You make it routine to engage in acts of purposeful self-care.

ENGAGE IN SELF-CARE

Focusing on yourself makes self-care possible. Self-care means being mindfully aware of your needs and taking action to restore or increase well-being and health, both physical and psychological.

Self-care is essential to living a wholehearted life, filled with confidence and overflowing with love and care for others. It is often said that you cannot pour from an empty vessel. In that spirit, self-care fills your own cup first and enables you to care for others from that abundance.

Self-care is often confused with self-indulgence, but they are not the same. Self-care promotes well-being, while self-indulgence provides short-term satisfaction but may lead to neutral or negative longer-term outcomes. Self-care can be as simple as drinking enough water or as complex as instituting an empowering workout routine. It may be gentle, as when you meet your need for rest by going to bed early or take a day off to spend time in nature. It crosses the line to self-indulgence when such reprieves become too frequent and serve to avoid tasks, causing you added stress or financial impacts later. Self-care can look like a heartfelt conversation with a friend, while self-indulgence shows up in cheap, angry gossip. Self-care prompts you to eat good foods you enjoy when hungry until you are satisfied; self-indulgence polishes off an entire carton of ice cream.

Self-care embodies the truth that you are worthy. You don't need to wait for someone else to give you love; you can begin right now, today, by loving yourself in a variety of gentle ways. Taking time to invest in your own healing and growth, as you are doing by reading this book, is an act of self-care.

Self-care both flows from and reinforces self-love. It is the same kind of care you would provide for someone else you love. If you care for a child or another loved one, you probably feed them nourishing foods and ensure that they have enough, create routines that allow for enough sleep, provide opportunities for physical activity and socialization, show compassion when they are sad or hurt, and celebrate their successes. This can serve as a guide for your own self-care.

Self-care is radical. It turns on its head the cultural and gaslighting lies that you must change, becoming or doing something different to earn attention or affection. As you live out the truth of your intrinsic worth, you reject the lie that deserving kindness is a goal to achieve. In quiet subversion, you defy the limitations gaslighting has imposed.

WORK ON SELF-ESTEEM

Low self-esteem can present a barrier to the self-care that you deserve and need. If you felt an inner resistance while reading the previous section, your battered heart may need healing around the question of your worth. Undermining your self-esteem is pivotal to the gaslighter's schemes; a less secure you can be more readily manipulated and controlled. It is no wonder, then, that so many people who have endured ongoing gaslighting sustain damage to their self-esteem.

Addressing diminished self-esteem is essential to taking back your life from the gaslighter's control. Spend some time in self-reflection. How do you feel about yourself? Be honest. When you look in the mirror or when you picture yourself approaching a group of people, what stories do you inwardly tell about yourself?

If you readily access a list of perceived flaws, try shifting that inner narrative with "even though" language. For example, "Even though I don't like my acne/wrinkles/size/shape/appearance of a certain body part, I wholly and completely accept myself." Or try "Even though I wish I had a higher education/more interesting job, these things do not define me or my worth." Such cognitive reframing will not change your feelings overnight, but as you rehearse new mantras, you will gradually retrain your brain to form new neural pathways that lead you out of self-loathing and into self-esteem.

If your gaslighting experience was traumatic, it may take more than cognitive retraining to make this essential internal shift. When low self-esteem is attached to specific painful memories, those memories may need reprocessing at a deeper level. There is no shame in this. Recognizing when you are stuck is important so you know when to seek out a skilled therapist who can help you overcome these painful sticking points with a brain-based trauma approach.

BUILD CONFIDENCE

Self-esteem is enhanced by building confidence and creating an empowered sense of self. As you build self-confidence, you will find a greater ability to recognize and stand up against gaslighting. You will find the strength to resist the influence of gaslighting, to trust and assert your truth, and to set boundaries as needed for your own well-being.

There are many avenues to building self-confidence. Physical activities can be especially empowering. Consider trying a dance class, martial arts, or yoga. All these options provide routes to embodiment of self, giving you permission to take up space in the world, to learn that growth is progressive, that mistakes are acceptable, and that you only need to measure yourself against yourself. As you gain skill, you will likely notice a sense of confidence begin to flourish, both in the studio and flowing out into your life.

For others, physical limitations may lead in a different direction. Groups such as Toastmasters provide opportunities to develop skills and confidence in the art of public speaking within a supportive group environment. Music is another powerful mode of self-expression, inner regulation, and confidence building. Consider learning an instrument, joining a choir, or taking voice lessons.

Even subtle shifts can change your outlook and sense of self in the world. Practice shifting your inner self-talk from messages of "I can't" or "I will fail" to affirmations of "I can do this," "My best is good enough," or "I am learning and growing, and that is okay." Be conscious of your body posture, rolling your shoulders back to open your chest, lifting your chin, and relaxing the worry lines around your eyes and mouth and across your forehead. Try it now and notice the corresponding emotive shift. Our bodies are intricately interconnected with our minds.

BUILD TRUST WITH YOURSELF

After a prolonged period of living in a state of anxiety and self-doubt, it can be difficult to trust yourself and feel safe again. Your nervous system becomes accustomed to living in a heightened, hypervigilant state and remains on alert to protect you. This shows up in insomnia, tense muscles, constant worry, quickened heartbeat, and shallow breathing. For some, the nervous system becomes exhausted and depleted, leaving you de-energized and out of touch with your intuition, which is reflected in depression.

It is necessary to reregulate your emotions from these excessive highs or lows into what psychiatrist Daniel Siegel calls the "window of tolerance" in his book *The Developing Mind.* In this more moderate zone, your inner wisdom or intuition becomes useful again. You can tolerate warning signals or sadness without overwhelming distress, listen to such emotions, and act mindfully upon what they are telling you. You can process historical triggers associated with present feelings of lack of safety with therapies like EMDR or Brainspotting; this may be a necessary and liberating gift you can give yourself toward this goal.

Gentle physical activity is another route to building internal trust. Yoga has been found to induce a lasting calming influence on the nervous system, while providing an avenue to increasing interoception, or awareness of sensations in the body, according to research from Dr. Bessel van der Kolk's Trauma Center. The keener your interoception, the better equipped you are to receive the subtle cues your body gives you as intuitive knowledge. When you trust yourself, you reclaim a sense of safety.

Another way to build trust with yourself is to give focused attention to your thoughts. It may be helpful to journal your thoughts, feelings, and observations. After writing, go over what you wrote and use different colored highlighters to differentiate "what I feel," "what I think," and "what I know." Allow yourself confidence and authority to sit with that distinction: There are things you *know* to be true. You can trust that. Give yourself permission to explore the ideas and fears your instinct suggests, holding them loosely and with humility, yet not dismissing them outright, either. Your intuition is wiser than you may know.

If you continue to have gaslighters or suspected gaslighters in your life, whether in close relationships or at a distance, you may benefit from bringing witnesses and taking notes, perhaps even in front of them, to reference later. This not only can help set boundaries that discourage lies, manipulation, and gaslighting but importantly helps restore confidence in your own perceptions. When the gaslighter denies what they have said, but you can cross-reference the conversation to your notes or witnesses, you build trust with yourself and reclaim power from the manipulator.

KEEP CHECKING IN

You have learned a lot of skills so far to increase your self-awareness, self-confidence, and self-knowledge. Continue to check in with yourself regularly, making it a life habit rather than merely an exercise in a book. Slow down and pause, scan your body, and check in with your emotions daily, perhaps several times each day. This can be a good way to start or end a day and a good periodic check-in, too. If you notice yourself becoming agitated, pause and turn inward, exploring what that may be about.

Simply notice what you are feeling and accept it with absolute compassion. Explore whether your feelings are guiding you toward any action, boundary, or self-care task. Notice where you are within the window of tolerance, and consider what steps you may need or want to take to restore yourself to balance. Know that you are worthy.

AN ONGOING PROCESS

As you worked your way through this chapter, perhaps you noticed how everything is interconnected: compassion, self-knowledge, self-love, self-care, self-esteem, confidence, and the ability to trust yourself depend and build upon one another. Healing and growth are a process. You cannot rush it, but you can deepen the work by extending grace and patience to yourself along the way. It may feel difficult, or even silly, but simply notice the resistance of your inner critic and gently dismiss its negative voice. Allow yourself this time, space, and compassion to grow, heal, and strengthen.

As you implement these steps, perhaps rereading them from time to time, you will start to notice small changes. As you review past journal entries, you may notice a shift and recognize that when you weren't even aware, change was happening. You are releasing pain, embracing healing, and finding freedom.

The following exercises will help reinforce the healing work you've begun as you worked through this step. Take your time to work through each exercise mindfully. You can revisit them anytime you need to.

EXERCISE 1: PEACEFUL PLACE

This exercise is used in EMDR therapy. It is a useful resource to help restore emotional balance when feeling overwhelmed.

Think of a place that feels peaceful. This may be somewhere you have been before or a place from your imagination. Think of somewhere that feels calm and serene when you picture yourself there alone.

Find your place in the scene. What do you see around you? What are the colors? Are you sitting, standing, or lying down? What does the surface beneath you feel like? Imagine the warmth of the sand, the coolness of the grass, or the sturdy support of the rock or wood or chair. What do you smell in this place? Salty air? Woodsy pine? What sounds can you hear? What does the sun or breeze feel like against your skin? Or are you indoors, with a soft, cozy blanket wrapped around you?

Notice what happens in your body as you immerse yourself in this scene. How has your breathing changed? Have your muscles relaxed? Did your posture shift? Notice how that feels.

With your eyes gently closed, stay here as long as feels right. Let yourself soak in what you need. When you are ready, you can return to your daily tasks, knowing that your peaceful place is there to return to whenever you need it.

EXERCISE 2: RESCRIPTING NEGATIVE SELF-TALK

To begin silencing the inner critic, familiarize yourself with its most common attacks. Take some time to counter this negativity with words of truth and empowerment.

Negative Ideas I Tell Myself:	Replacement Truths:
I can't do anything right.	I may not be great at everything, but I am good at some things and am learning.

It may be helpful to write out some of your replacement truths on cue cards or sticky notes and put them in places you will frequently see. Repeat them until they come naturally!

EXERCISE 3: SELF-CARE STRATEGY

Fill in the boxes with at least one idea each of ways you can care for yourself.

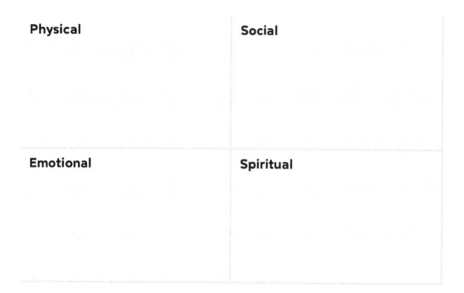

Physical

Social

Emotional

Spiritual

You have begun something very important in the stillness of this step. Learning to love yourself is foundational to cultivating healthy and satisfying relationships. Building upon your growing self-awareness and self-confidence, let's consider how to establish healthy boundaries that support the self-care you deserve and desire.

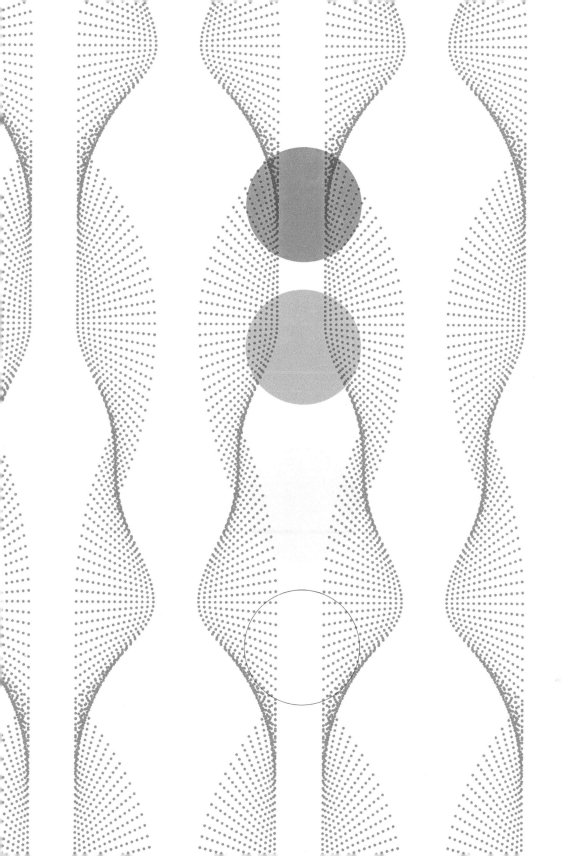

STEP 5:
BUILD
HEALTHY
BOUNDARIES

Having given yourself the time, space, and care to grow in your self-awareness, self-esteem, and self-confidence, you have laid the groundwork for the important step of building healthy boundaries. Notice any internal resistance you are feeling to the ideas represented by the topic of this step. Now go back to what you have learned and know to be true of yourself: You matter. Your self-care is essential. You deserve to be seen and to be treated with kindness and respect. Let's explore how to cultivate space around you that fosters these dynamics.

WHAT ARE BOUNDARIES?

Boundaries are concrete actions we take to protect our emotional and physical space. Boundaries may be communicated and enforced through words as well as behavior and often require both types of action. You might tell someone, "I'm happy to talk on the phone, but I am not available after 9:00 p.m." This verbal communication is reinforced by shutting off your phone or ignoring calls and texts after that time of night.

Boundaries are essential to healthy relationships because they protect your energy, allowing you to maintain self-care and show up for others without letting these sometimes competing demands get out of balance. Without boundaries, relationships devolve into enmeshment, codependence, and even abuse.

It can take time and determination to establish boundaries. You may only gradually realize the need to enact a boundary as you increase your self-awareness. This may conflict with established patterns of behavior that have left you feeling depleted, exhausted, and overwhelmed. Creating new dynamics in a relationship can be like steering a large ship: it takes time for the efforts you set in motion to be recognized, understood, and respected. This demands consistency on your part as you remember your worth, value your needs, and persist in communication and action.

BOUNDARIES AND GASLIGHTING

Gaslighters hate boundaries. Boundaries protect you where gaslighters seek to exploit you. Sadistic gaslighters like to toy with you, and boundaries make you more resistant to their games. Narcissistic gaslighters cultivate a reality in which they are the center, while boundaries honor your own space in the world and resist their hoovering. Boundaries repel manipulation.

Not only does enacting boundaries protect you in your current and future relationships, it also makes space in your life for people who will honor your needs and wants. Gaslighters home in on people they perceive as weak or easily manipulated and won't waste time beginning a relationship with someone who demonstrates this pattern of assertive self-worth.

Setting a boundary that you will only speak to the gaslighter with a third party present can provide a level of protection and validation and interrupt the crazy-making cycle. The third party can help you process the insidious manipulations later while serving as an essential anchor to your sense of reality. Alternatively, you may set a standard that you will take notes, record conversations, or insist upon written communication.

When you begin to set boundaries with a gaslighter who's been established in your life for some time, expect resistance. Their goal is to control you to serve their own needs, and your boundaries will threaten that. The gaslighter may escalate the tactics we've reviewed, but you'll be better prepared now that you know what they are. At these moments, anticipate rage, self-pity, hoovering, ghosting, and stonewalling. Know that these manipulations are aimed at destroying your boundaries and regaining control.

HOW YOU'VE BEEN CONDITIONED TO SEE BOUNDARIES

Setting boundaries is difficult for many people. It is often associated with pushing others away, being selfish, or being unloving. For those who have been raised as parentified children—made to act as caregivers for their parents rather than the other way around—boundaries constitute an act of rebellion against the "good child" narrative. You may have grown up in an enmeshed household where there is little sense of where you end and the parent begins, where there is no permission to grow and fulfill the appropriate developmental tasks of pursuing autonomy and independence. Many have been raised in authoritarian households where some version of the refrain "Don't you say no to me!" was ingrained. When saying no is equated with being "bad," boundaries are quashed before they can develop.

Such repressive messages can be reinforced throughout many spheres of life. Controlling friends, partners, religious institutions, or bosses are likely to run over your limits and press for more than you have to give. They may overrule your understanding of appropriate relationship boundaries with gaslighting narratives of what it means to love, serve, worship, or perform appropriately. Such gaslighters frequently use guilt to entrap and corral.

To take a meaningful look at boundaries, it is necessary to examine your values and beliefs about selflessness and selfishness. If you've been shamed into believing that taking care of your own needs is selfish, or that your needs don't matter, setting boundaries will be a challenge. For many women in particular, social conditioning contributes to shaping the false perception that a good woman gives endlessly and without limit. If, in your experience, love was entangled with conditions, saying no can feel terrifying, risking the relationship itself. Know that healthy relationships are not transactional. You can have limits and still be valued or loved.

WHY IT'S OKAY TO SET LIMITS

Setting boundaries communicates who we are and what we need to others. Healthy people do not want to take advantage of you and could misinterpret your lack of resistance, thinking that nothing is wrong. For example, if you always accept every assignment your boss gives you without comment even when overwhelmed, they cannot necessarily be faulted for assuming that you are simply a high performer who can handle it. If you always agree to babysit your nephews, how would your sister know that you are burnt out for lack of free time? Without such communication, resentment can build and harm what might otherwise be a strong relationship. Communicating boundaries demonstrates respect for the other person as well as for yourself.

A gaslighter will meet boundaries with resistance. This can serve as a litmus test for the health of the relationship. Such resistance is not reason to back down. If you constantly give, fail to assert your needs, and allow mistreatment, you risk burnout, emotional depletion, and lowered self-esteem. You deserve better.

Healthy relationships involve giving as well as receiving. If the energy and effort are heavily weighted in one direction, it may indicate a lack of and need for boundary assertion.

Limits don't have to be harsh. In relationships with healthy people, you can create permeable boundaries. If a boundary is a wall, you can add doors and give keys to trusted people who have proven themselves respectful of your boundaries. For example, you may have set aside time on Saturday mornings to be your "me time" for reading, working out, or doing something else that fills your spirit. Perhaps there are a few select friends for whom you would adjust that boundary if they needed you, knowing that they would not take advantage. Creating boundaries does not mean shutting out love.

STARTING FROM SCRATCH

Perhaps you've warmed to the idea that boundaries can be good, but you don't know where to start. Let's take a look at creating new boundaries uniquely designed to fit you, your needs, your life circumstances, and your relationships. Consider the following sections with mindful curiosity to help determine what boundaries may be needed in your life.

Healthy Boundaries in Action

Let's take a look at some tangible examples of what boundary setting may look like in real life.

Mario and Rosa had been arguing a lot. The minute Mario got home, Rosa started into him with accusations and verbal attacks. Mario clenched and unclenched his fists, then took a deep breath and asserted, "Rosa, I'm not willing to argue in front of the kids. We can talk about this later." As Rosa continued to call him names, Mario glanced at their kids' wide-eyed faces and steeled his resolve. "Later, Rosa. I'm going to take a shower now." He kissed his son on the forehead, ruffled his daughter's hair, went into the bathroom, and locked the door.

• • •

Aisha was shaking when she hung up the phone with her mom. She stared out the window for a few minutes, then texted her sister. "Ebony, I need you to talk to me directly when you're upset with me, not complain to Mom. I love you, and I want our relationship to be open and direct."

• • •

Having come to recognize his coworker Bella's patterns as gaslighting, Ahmad knew he had to make some changes if he was going to continue in the job he loved. "Bella," Ahmad said, "I find myself frequently confused by what I remember you telling me and what you report to our boss. Going forward, I'm not willing to go over project data with you without another team member present. I'll also be taking notes to help ensure the accuracy of my memory."

THINK ABOUT YOUR OWN NEEDS

Effective boundaries emerge from recognized needs. Your needs matter, and you are the person best positioned to protect them. If you need time to study, alone time with your immediate family, more sleep, emotional safety without having to deflect racist or ableist jokes, or advance notice if the babysitter is going to cancel, the only way to have these needs met is through setting a boundary verbally and following through with action. Wishing, complaining, and resenting will not achieve what you need.

In a healthy relationship, there is room for your needs to coexist with those of the other person. You neither demand that the other person meet all your needs, nor do you habitually deny your own needs to become everything that they want. You do not make yourself small in order to earn acceptance or affection.

GET IN TOUCH WITH YOUR FEELINGS

How do you feel when you are responding to the demands, requests, needs, guilt trips, or other manipulations of the gaslighter? How would you feel if you did not do the thing they want? Would you be afraid of their reaction or of losing closeness?

Your feelings matter. While we do make sacrifices in close relationships, if the demands for sacrifice are constant and leave you feeling exhausted, depleted, and resentful, something is out of balance. If imagining not having to do the things expected of you provides a scent of freedom, boundaries are presently lacking.

Check in with yourself regularly. Notice your feelings. What are they telling you? Listen to them.

CONSIDER WHAT YOU ARE COMFORTABLE WITH

Putting aside for now the question of how the other person would react, imagine a world in which you felt full permission and autonomy to decide how you show up in this relationship. Consider what you are comfortable with regarding communication mode, frequency, and time, how they speak to you and about you, disclosure of your secrets to others, topics broached, time spent together, time spent apart, physical touch or sex if applicable, and personal space. If you have a relationship with a gaslighter, it is a safe bet that you are not comfortable with the dynamics in some of these areas.

Let yourself imagine, without self-censorship, a relationship in which your preferences in these areas were followed. There is no right answer here, as boundaries flow from self-knowledge and are as unique as your own personality. Your level of introversion or extroversion may impact what boundaries you set, but it does not determine whether or not boundaries are needed. The degree to which you are a structured or free-spirited person may likewise influence how rigid or malleable your boundaries are, yet every-one has needs that deserve to be communicated and respected.

GIVE YOURSELF PERMISSION

As you read and consider these questions, you may be gaining a sense of where boundaries need to be established or strength-ened in your personal life. You might even have ideas of what those boundaries could look like, what you'd like to say, or how you might back up such boundaries with action. The critical next step is giving yourself permission.

Take a moment to reflect on the fears or anxieties that hold you back. What is the cost that you fear paying should you vocal-ize the limits you need? How realistic is it that you would pay that price? What cost do you suffer already by failing to establish or reinforce boundaries?

Boundary enactment is an act of self-care. Know that you are worthy of the emotional, physical, and psychological protection that boundaries provide. Give yourself permission to choose you.

WHAT IS TOO MUCH TOO SOON?

In establishing new relationships, pay attention to pacing. Gas-lighters have a tendency to rapidly escalate relationships with effusive displays of adoration. Be wary of premature declarations of love, pressure for physical intimacy, or early discussions of a shared future with a new date. Keep an eye on new acquain-tances who quickly declare that you are their best friend forever and quickly begin to text all day, every day. Be cautious of groups that immediately promote you to positions of unearned responsibility or leadership, such as a church that suggests a new member teach the children's class.

Consider what feels comfortable and appropriate. While gushing expressions of admiration can boost your self-esteem, these behaviors are a warning sign of a lack of boundaries and potential smothering and control. In healthy relationships, you can expect time to reflect on your experience with the person or institution and let your own intuition guide you forward or away.

Self-Awareness and Boundaries

While it is important to have solid boundaries around important values emanating from a strong sense of self, some boundaries may be more fluid. With self-awareness of your changing needs and energy levels, give yourself permission to assert your needs and set up situational, temporary boundaries. This can look like a general boundary of principle, such as "I will not visit my in-laws when I am feeling exhausted." In action, this boundary is expressed in response to regular internal check-ins and communicated in a non-blaming, self-assertive manner: "I'm sorry, I won't be able to join you for dinner tonight. I look forward to seeing you next week."

PRACTICE ASSERTIVENESS

Boundary setting requires assertiveness. But before you skip the rest of the chapter because that's "not you," recognize that assertiveness is a skill and can be developed. Assertion comes from a grounded sense of self and knowing your worth and your right to speak up.

Assertiveness is *not* aggression. It is the sweet spot between passivity, in which you lack boundaries out of a felt need to be perceived as "nice," and aggression, in which you disregard others' boundaries and rights out of a desire to have your way. Assertiveness means speaking firmly, confidently, and calmly about what you need or want.

Assertiveness can work with different communication styles; there is no one correct script. It does require self-awareness, directness, and communication of your authentic self. It can be challenging for those who have been continually emotionally abused and gaslit and who are consequently coming from a place of diminished self-confidence and increased self-doubt.

It may be intimidating to imagine establishing new boundaries in a relationship where your feelings and rights have long been violated. You can work your way up to this in lower-consequence scenarios. For example, in a restaurant, when your order is incorrect, practice assertion by respectfully identifying the problem and requesting that the mistaken item be replaced, rather than quietly eating the unwanted meal or going hungry. Notice any anxiety this act brings up, reassure yourself that you have the right to be assertive, and move through the discomfort. Work on setting assertive boundaries with a friend who asks for recreational time when you are busy. Rather than carving time out of your much-needed sleep, try "I would love to spend time with you, but I can't tonight. Can we try again next weekend?" As you gain confidence speaking for yourself in these lower-stakes scenarios without becoming angry or backing down, and as you notice that the reactions you fear tend not to materialize, you can begin flexing these new muscles in your more challenging relationships.

DEALING WITH GUILT AND FEAR

The biggest challenge in setting boundaries is often fear of others' reactions. You may feel guilty for saying no because you don't want to let anyone down. You may fear that they will withdraw love, respect, the possibility of work promotion, or the relationship itself. You may anticipate anger.

Above all, remember that you are not responsible for others' emotions. Because you are a caring person, it may be hard to accept that someone could feel disappointment or hurt when you set limits. But you can hold a boundary and empathize with their disappointment without having to rescue them from their feelings or contort yourself in an effort to alleviate those feelings.

When others react with a victim mentality or lash out in anger, they are displaying their own lack of appropriate boundaries. Your only responsibility is to recognize and assert your own needs, which can be done with kindness and compassion and as much firmness as necessary.

While it is not your job to mollify anyone, you know your own situation best. If you know or intuit that it could be unsafe for you to say no or set limits in your relationship due to the risk of violence, you will need to create physical safety and distance first. Boundary setting is not a negotiation. Your boundary may need to be expressed as a conclusion rather than an if/then scenario. Nevertheless, you continue to back up the boundary with action. Instead of words/action, you create an action sandwich: action/words/action. For example, one assertive boundary may look like "I am not comfortable having you discuss my weight. I will end this call if you continue." For others, where safety is in question, the boundary may need to be "I have decided to leave you. I am staying somewhere safe and will not be returning. If you continue to try to contact me, I will notify the police."

IT GETS EASIER

Identifying where boundaries would benefit you and what they might look like is a difficult but critical initial step. And it's only the beginning. Gaslighters will challenge you and try to erode any healthy boundaries you set up.

This is where all the work you have done is tested and where its value becomes apparent. Stand firm. Every boundary must be both verbalized and backed by action. Repeat your boundaries, and act on your words. If you said you would end the discussion if the language became abusive, end the discussion. If you noted that you are not available to work all weekend, do not work on the weekend. Your boundaries are good, and you deserve their protection.

It will get easier. After initial resistance, others usually respond to consistency by backing off the pressure. You gain confidence in your right and ability to assert your limits and begin to enjoy the benefits of protecting your emotional and physical space. This, in turn, makes it easier to resist the internal pressure to cave.

Enforcing personal boundaries will reshape your life, generally in a profoundly positive way. You may find more distance or even disconnection from people who only want to use or abuse you, and this may cycle you back to the grief step. But even as this shift takes place, you may draw others into your life by the confidence you exude in the boundaries you set. Your self-esteem will grow as you live out the truths that you are indeed worthy and valuable.

Perhaps, as you have worked your way through this step, you have some idea of areas where the gaslighter intrudes on you or fails to respect your personal space. The following exercises will help narrow the focus of these concepts into actionable steps to analyze, prepare, and create boundaries that will enhance your well-being and become an important, ongoing act of self-care.

EXERCISE 1: ASSESS PRESENT BOUNDARIES

Take a moment to consider the current state of your boundaries. For each category, rate your boundary setting and enforcement by checking the appropriate box.

	Weak	Healthy	Rigid
Social			
Emotional			
Physical			
Sexual			
Material			
Time			

EXERCISE 2: IDENTIFY BLOCKING BELIEFS

Consider your inner voice and the fears that hold you back from the boundaries that you desire. List your negative beliefs about limit setting on the left and counter them on the right.

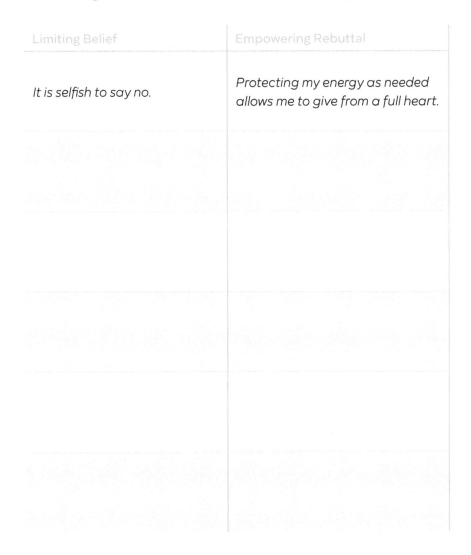

Limiting Belief	Empowering Rebuttal
It is selfish to say no.	*Protecting my energy as needed allows me to give from a full heart.*

EXERCISE 3: DETERMINING BOUNDARIES

It's time for the essential step of identifying new boundaries or shoring up existing boundary ideals with plans of action. For each domain, identify a boundary that would reinforce your well-being. Then write down the words you could use to communicate it and actions you will take to back it up.

	Words	Actions
Social		
Emotional		
Physical		
Sexual		
Material		
Time		

As you worked through this step and the exercises, you may have wondered about safety, practicality, and whether the gaslighter will respect your boundaries. You may even be questioning whether it is worth it. You do deserve to reap the benefits of boundaries in your life, regardless of whom you allow into your inner circle. Holding on to the important work you have done here, let's now explore the question of ongoing contact in greater depth as we turn to the sixth step toward breaking free.

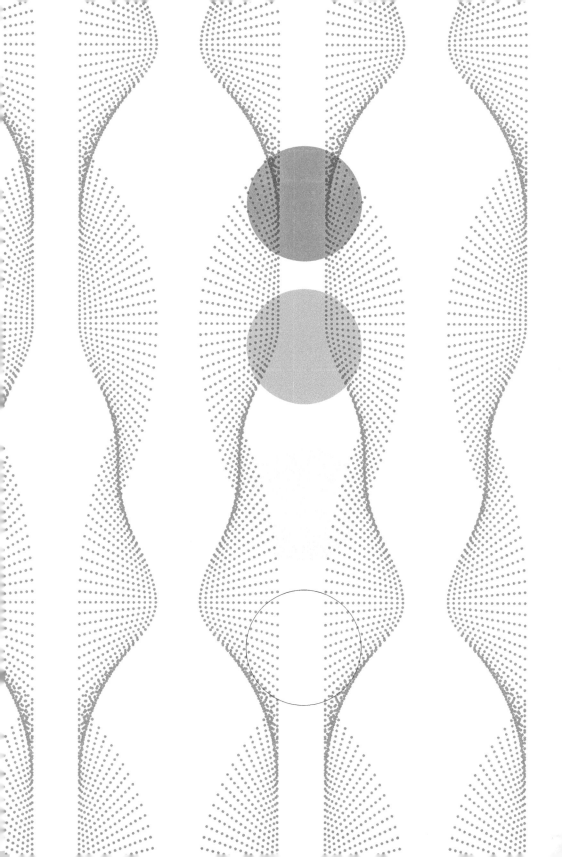

STEP 6:
MAKE
DECISIONS

Boundaries, as we discussed in the previous step, delineate the distance and parameters at which you can have a healthy relationship with both yourself and others simultaneously. But what happens when others won't respect that distance or space? Perhaps the idea of cutting contact is appealing. Let's explore that potential and whether it is necessary, wise, or a possibility in your unique situation.

DECISIONS

Perhaps you have tried setting boundaries with the gaslighter, and no matter how you try to back up your limits with action, they continue to disrespect your personal emotional and physical space. Or maybe you intuitively know that to set healthy boundaries would lead to violence against you. You might desperately wish to break ties but are entangled due to financial pressures, pets, children, or other interconnected family relationships. Maybe you just aren't sure yet whether a relationship with boundaries is enough or whether you'd like to cut contact entirely. This chapter will explore these complicated questions and scenarios to help you gain clarity and make decisions that will support your well-being.

YOU CAN'T PREVENT SOMEONE FROM GASLIGHTING YOU

As we work through the steps toward breaking free from gas-lighting, you may have noticed one topic missing: how to stop the gaslighter. The truth is that you cannot fix anyone else. No one changes who doesn't intrinsically want to change. And most important, you are not responsible for anyone else's choices or behavior, not even when it targets you.

Accepting the limits of your own control is an important part of finding where your power *is*. You can identify the problem, label it, and understand it. You can be savvy and self-aware. You can set limits on what you will accept. But ultimately, you can't control how the gaslighter will respond. What you can do is take care of yourself, find safety, and if you have others depending on you, keep them safe as well.

FINDING CLOSURE

When a significant relationship is coming to its end, it is natural to seek a sense of closure. Closure means finding clarity as to why the relationship is ending, releasing emotional turmoil over the separation, and allowing space for new relationships to arise and thrive. When you are the one to end a relationship, the first goal of gaining clarity comes more easily, but it's important to spend some time reflecting on it to find a deep, true sense of closure.

You may cycle back to grief again; this is not regression but a deeper layer of release and healing. Just as when you climb a spiral staircase, you circle around again, yet you continue to rise. Closure demands a process in which you release your inner pain over what is not and will not be. Allow yourself to feel that pain, to name those regrets, to identify that hurt so you can release it.

In cultivating closure, let yourself internalize the good you have received from this complicated relationship and give thanks for that, either spiritually or directly. Then allow yourself to also iden-tify the harm and refuse to receive that anymore. In so doing, you can let go.

A final and voluntary act of closure comes in the shape of forgiveness. Forgiveness does not mean condoning negative actions or allowing harm to continue, nor does it negate their impact on you. It simply means that you release what was and give up resentment and desire for revenge. Forgiveness means that, even as you cut ties, you no longer allow the other person's past actions to impact your present or future. Forgiveness is for you, to be set free.

CLOSURE IS ABOUT YOU

Closure is a process you must foster in and for yourself. Don't wait for closure from the gaslighter. Their goal is to control you; they will not readily help you let go. Closure is not about the gaslighter changing. They do not have to accept your limits or your goodbye. You still have the authority to decide what you want in your life, with or without their permission. Your closure must not depend on that.

So how do you develop a sense of closure if they will not help facilitate it? One important element of closure is developing a coherent self-driven narrative about your relationship and what happened between you. This is particularly important—and challenging—in emerging from a gaslighting relationship where your reality was constantly disputed. Tell your story. Write it down, tell it to a friend, or work through it with a therapist. Stories make sense of our lived experience, helping us put the past in its place and leave it behind.

As you work through this, ask yourself: are they the person you imagined they would be? It's time to let go of unrealistic expectations and grapple with what is. It can be helpful, instead, to focus on the positive outcomes of the separation.

For many people, there may be a sense of unfinished business. The empty chair technique may help you find closure. Find some privacy and set up a chair across from you. Picture the gaslighter sitting there. Notice how that feels. Mindfully observe what words come up that you would like to say to them. Remember that you are safe; they cannot hurt you. Give yourself permission to speak aloud all the things you wish you could say, until there is nothing left.

An alternative approach is to write a letter to the gaslighter. Depending on the dynamics and safety in your relationship, you might give them the letter, or simply write it for your own closure process. Spend four or more days writing it, until all the things you need to say are spent. Then close the letter and breathe. You may wish to write a second condensed version to share, or simply leave it folded and tucked away for your own purposes of release. Remember, closure is for you alone.

NO CONTACT

Once you've found closure, don't keep checking up on the gaslighter. Block their number and disconnect on social media. Let the door remain closed. You have made a decision and crossed that threshold. There is no reason to go back.

Gaslighters tend to have a level of personality pathology that is unlikely to change. They will hoover you back into the cycle of love-bombing, devaluation, and discarding if you give them the chance, just to avoid being the one who lost. Don't play their ego games.

When a dangerous gaslighter unleashes their flying monkeys to coerce you back, you may face a second round of difficult decisions. If such people are firmly aligned with the gaslighter and will not respect your boundaries, you might decide to cut or strictly limit contact with them as well. This can be even more difficult than the decision to cut contact with the gaslighter, depending on the depth of your relationship with these people. When the flying monkeys are your family or friends, you face another layer of grief. As you move through these decisions, hold fast to the truth that you deserve the peace that you are cultivating for yourself. You deserve to be free.

What Would Your Life Look Like without the Gaslighter?

If you close your eyes and picture life without the gaslighter, what do you see? How do you feel? What would be different? Where would you be? Allow yourself time to explore these questions and just sit with them. If anxiety arises, explore that: What aspect feels scary? Is it a fear you want to give in to or one you'd like to conquer? Perhaps you are surprised to experience a sense of freedom or relief. Notice that, too. There's no right answer to these questions.

A study published in the *Journal of Experimental Social Psychology* on breakup distress found that people consistently overestimated the negative feelings they anticipated when contemplating ending a relationship. It may be easier than you think. Listen to your heart; there's wisdom there.

WHEN YOU CAN'T GO NO-CONTACT

The hard line of no contact may not be an option for you. There may be legal or practical realities that keep you tied. Complicated family ties may make highly structured boundaries more appropriate than zero contact, and perhaps this is sufficient for you. You might need to maintain contact for a time, with an eventual parting on the horizon.

The simplest scenario, though still not easy emotionally, is in the friendship or relationship without shared children or pets. The emotional entanglements are real, but concrete ties are few. Employment scenarios are more complicated, because pragmatic realities may demand a waiting period before cutting contact as you look for alternate work or persist toward retirement. The greatest complications arise in family scenarios. Elderly parents may be dependent upon you or critical to valued connections with siblings. Spouses and partners with whom you share child custody are likely to be the most complicated of all.

WHAT IF CHILDREN ARE INVOLVED?

It is not uncommon to stay in an unhealthy or toxic relationship "for the kids." Although self-sacrifice is noble, it is important to critically analyze whether staying is truly altruistic or may be causing you and the children further harm. When children see emotional abuse modeled as their pattern for a "normal" relationship, they are much more likely to follow this example in their own adult relationships. Further, it's likely that if you are being emotionally abused, the children are, too. If they are witnessing or absorbing signs of domestic violence, they are suffering psychological harm. This is not something to tolerate to keep the family together.

If you decide to leave, you will most likely remain entangled through child custody arrangements. If this becomes your reality, establishing and enforcing firm boundaries will be essential. Consultation with an attorney or public legal aid is highly recommended, even at the contemplation stage.

WHAT IF PETS ARE INVOLVED?

With both children and pets, shared custody works best in amicable separations. If you have determined that a breakup is necessary, you face the difficult decision of whether the toxic relationship is worth continued contact with your furry companions. If no prenuptial agreement is in place, the pet is usually considered the legal property of the one who paid for them. It may not be possible to work out an agreeable custody sharing arrangement. Even if the gaslighter is willing to do so, consider that this provides an avenue for continual gaslighting, manipulation, cruelty, and hoovering you back into their clutches. Depending on the gaslighter's level of sadism, keeping this door open through shared custody could threaten the safety of your beloved pet. Proceed with caution.

Should you conclude that you need to leave the abusive relationship and you have no legal right to take your pet with you, and the gaslighter is not willing to let you keep them, you will undoubtedly face a secondary layer of grief that is real, deep, and painful. Allow yourself to grieve that loss, working through the stages of grief. There is no easy way around this. Allowing the pet to remain may be the kindest grace you can give them as you create safety for yourself. If they are endangering the pet, do call the police. Most of all, do not doubt that your right to a life shaped by respect and safety comes first.

LIMITED CONTACT

For these and other complex reasons, limited contact may be your best option. This may involve setting boundaries, such as "I will only meet with you in a neutral, public location for up to one hour." A friendship with shared school, church, or club membership associations may be limited by drawing firm boundaries around when and where each participates at the facility.

An ex-partner with shared custody may best be managed through limiting modes of communication, such as "I will only communicate via email, which I will check in the evenings. I will write no more than one email per day. Phone contact is only to be used in emergencies." If the gaslighter continues to violate the boundary, it may be reinforced by blocking text messages or hanging up on nonemergency phone calls.

The variety of relationships and the challenges to curating the limited contact you desire are myriad. What is important to recognize is that there *are* solutions that will move you closer to your goal. You deserve freedom, and you can create space and time in your life free of emotional abuse.

What If the Gaslighter Promises to Change?

You know you should leave but . . . you love them. What if they promise to change? Might you be giving up too soon? It's a sincere and loving wish, but it's little more than that. As we've discussed, no one changes who does not intrinsically want to. You can't make someone else change.

There are a few scenarios where this might be different. The gaslighter may have experienced some kind of "rock bottom" wake-up call. Ironically, the very act of leaving may be such an experience. Nevertheless, be cautious of gaslighters who would feign change in order to hoover you back in. You have the right to leave without looking back.

So how do you know whether a professed change is real? Ask yourself what is concretely different from every other time they have promised change. Have they undertaken individual therapy of their own accord? If so, has such therapy focused on healing the underlying wounds that shaped this manipulative behavior? Couples therapy, or therapy where they focus on complaining about you, will not suffice.

Do you see evidence of change, or do they simply claim to be different? Was the change overnight, or has time passed showing sustained change? Vulnerability and raw honesty are essential to and markers of change. When change is genuine, you'll see introspective reflection and specific remorse. Sincere apologies take responsibility, are specific, and do not suggest shared blame. Such changes are extraordinarily unlikely from the sadistic or narcissistic gaslighter but may be possible with a defensive/insecure gaslighter.

You can hold compassion for them while maintaining compassion for yourself. If you do not see these markers of change, love yourself enough to maintain healthy distance.

PLANNING YOUR EXIT

Leaving Max was not going to be easy. Scarlett felt sure he had others watching her and knew he tracked her phone. He controlled the online profile where she solicited dates, and the money went straight into his account, from which he paid her rent. Even though she didn't live with him, she was constantly under his thumb.

Scarlett had first seen the number for the sex trafficking hotline on the inside of a bathroom stall door. It was easy to memorize: 888-3737-888. She repeated it over and over until one day, she made the call and spoke to a woman who provided concrete guidance, resources, and hope.

Scarlett set a day to leave Max and her old life behind. She knew there could be no gradual transition or negotiation, so she left, purposely leaving two crucial things inside: the key and the phone. There would be no going back. She stepped into the waiting car as with any date and stared straight ahead as they drove off, heading to the safe house.

Leaving a gaslighter is an intentional act. You've assessed the situation and determined that the relationship is emotionally abusive, and that the feeling that you are crazy or hysterical is all just part of the game. You know that this relationship can't continue.

But leaving will look different based on a variety of factors unique to your circumstances. Scarlett's departure was precarious, though simplified by a lack of children. Others may face less danger yet grapple with complicating factors involving finances or interconnected secondary relationships. Even if the relationship with the gaslighter didn't emerge organically, as with a parent or sibling, gaslighters are skilled at infiltrating multiple areas of your life to make control more complete.

Let's explore some alternative approaches to leaving for those for whom a sudden, clean break is not the best or preferred approach.

THE SLOW FADE

The slow fade can be a useful approach to extricating yourself from a friendship with a gaslighter. It is not appropriate for relationships involving domestic violence. It can be useful when leaving an organization about which you have conflicted feelings of loyalty and dread, such as a religious organization or club. In such circumstances, you owe no explanation. You can simply decrease and space out contact, holding firm to your own boundaries until the person or organization no longer has a space in your life.

This approach is particularly useful if you are unsure whether tightening boundaries or ending contact is the action you wish to take. In general, direct communication is best, being authentic, courageous, and respectful. However, the slow fade can precede such honesty by letting you test out an experience of less or no contact with the gaslighter in your life.

BEING DIRECT

In most circumstances in which you do not face a physical threat, it is best to be direct. For example, if you have determined that your workplace involves unremitting gaslighting with which you no longer wish to grapple, it will become necessary to have a direct conversation ending the relationship—in this instance, your employment. You may plan this out, possibly by first securing another job. You can prepare for such difficult conversations by writing out what you want to say. You may need to discard your first draft, in which you express your hurt and anger, whittling it down to a shorter and more direct letter. It is not necessary to name or identify the gaslighting. Simply identify what is healthy for you, and take action to move away from what is unhealthy and toward what supports your well-being.

Direct conversations are also important in distancing yourself from unhealthy family by setting boundaries. It is less effective to leave them guessing as to what your new rules of engagement are. You will also need to be direct in ending an intimate relationship where you share a residence, unless you choose abrupt disappearance for safety reasons. In general, breakups are best when clear and direct.

DEALING WITH PUSHBACK

Expect pushback from the gaslighter. Their objective is, after all, to control you, and nothing breaks that power like ending the relationship. They may feel panicky or angry. They may yell, make promises, or threaten. They may dismiss your reasons for leaving, using their typical tactics of attacking your sanity, memory, or emotional stability.

To minimize pushback, simplify your explanations or offer none at all. You don't owe them a soft landing. Focus on yourself, identifying that you are making choices that are healthy for you. Be firm, calm, and persistent.

The gaslighter doesn't have to like your decision. You have made your choice, and just as with setting boundaries, you now reinforce your verbalized decision with action. You have that right. You get to walk away.

TALKING TO FRIENDS, FAMILY, AND OTHERS (IF YOU WANT TO)

When you decide to remove significant relationships from your life, you will likely face conversations with friends and family about these choices. You can try to circumvent unsolicited advice and opinions by prefacing any discussion with clear boundaries. You might say, "I have made a decision, and I want to tell you about it, but I'm not looking for input at this time." Attempts to sway you from decisions you have already made can be met with ending the conversation.

Give yourself time to begin processing your grief about the dissolution of your relationship before having any difficult conversations, so that you will feel stronger in standing firm. With supportive people, you may need less time, perhaps even sharing your thoughts and feelings throughout the process from acceptance to decision-making.

If children are involved, it is best to preface a move by communicating clearly with them, making room for their questions and concerns, while remaining resolute in what you know is best for yourself and them. However, it may be unwise to discuss with children plans to leave a violent gaslighter, due to the need to maintain security and prevent well-intentioned or accidental disclosures of your plan. In such a scenario, be sure to process feelings about the decision after the move, perhaps with the help of a child or family therapist.

As you discuss the life changes you are making, hold fast to your knowledge of what you need and deserve and your awakened understanding of the dynamics at play with the gaslighter. Be wary of the flying monkeys who do the gaslighter's bidding and may try to influence your conclusion. You know what is best for you, and you have the right to decide whom to allow within your sacred space.

TAPPING INTO YOUR SUPPORT NETWORK

While you can probably already picture the faces of those who might try to sway you from your resolution, don't be afraid to reach out to those who would extend support. Times of transition are difficult. You do not need to travel this road alone.

Don't be afraid to reach out to friends who may have become estranged by the gaslighter's schemes. Such relationships might need care, time, and work but may prove to be worth the vulnerability. Find your people, be authentic, and open yourself to their love and support. If you are unsure where to begin finding support, consider the resources at the back of this book, including hotlines and ways to locate a therapist who can help (page 149).

CARRY OUT YOUR PLAN

Once you have identified your support network, detailed a plan, and put into place any practical steps necessary, it is time to carry out your plan. This may be the hardest part of the entire process. Let yourself feel any inner resistance, fear, or sadness. Face it head-on, listen to it, note its shape and feel in your body, and let it subside. Then lift your chin, remember your value, and do what reinforces and supports that worth. You've got this.

WHEN GASLIGHTERS TRY TO GET BACK IN TOUCH

Gaslighters, by nature, are unlikely to simply let you go. Whether motivated by insecurity, where your retreat threatens their self-concept, or narcissism, which regards refusal as an insult, the very motives that drive gaslighters to their manipulative games compel them to resist release. Hoovering you back in is their all-too-common ploy.

It was a painful decision, but Ariel resolved to cut contact with her family. She realized now that their refusal to acknowledge what her stepfather had done to her throughout childhood created an unbearable tension for her. If, as they insisted, they had simply been a happy family, then all the blame for her teenage delinquency lay solely on her. Although she took responsibility for her choices, she was no longer willing to wear the "problem child" mantle.

Ariel wrote a brief, direct group email, informing them that she would not be attending their holiday gatherings any longer if it meant pretending what her stepfather did hadn't happened, in order to keep the peace. Ariel was afraid of the angry responses she might receive, but instead, she was met with silence . . . at first. As Thanksgiving approached, the calls, texts, and emails began. Her sister cajoled her to "let bygones be bygones." Her mother bemoaned spending the holidays without all her children. Her brother angrily scolded her for making the holidays all about her. Ariel's husband held her as she cried. Finally, he looked her in the eyes and asked, "What do you want to do?" Ariel drew a ragged breath and replied, "I'll respond to them all in January."

When boundaries are made clear but continue to be trespassed, you are faced with the difficult choice of giving in or fortifying through action. You must decide whether you are willing to walk away.

When Ariel's needs for recognition of her lived reality were ignored and met with continued gaslighting, she reinforced her stance with an unwavering silence. Their refusal to change made it clear that there was nothing left to be said. One cannot compromise or be complicit in being gaslit. There is no middle ground between truth and denial.

If your gaslighter tries, after a period of silence and peace, to get back in touch, critically evaluate: Is there evidence of change? Is it lasting and sustained? Do they own their past failures or pretend that nothing happened? Or are they simply cajoling you with appeals to your sentiments and loyalty? Although loyalty can be a lovely characteristic, you must first be true to yourself.

STAY STRONG AND BE CONSISTENT

Life without the gaslighter may feel empty at first. They've taken up so much space, pushing out others and demanding increasing time and attention for their needs. In the vacuum their presence leaves behind, you may feel hollow and alone.

Allow yourself to sit with that. Don't rush to avoid those feelings, filling up that space with food, shopping, alcohol, workaholism, or dates. Let yourself feel the void, noticing your feelings with gentle compassion, until you find yourself making peace with the change.

It is at this point when you may feel most tempted to invite or allow the gaslighter back into your life. You may talk yourself out of the resolute decision you made so boldly. Notice the negative voice criticizing and doubting your decisions and your authority over your own life. You may find yourself worrying about their feelings and berating yourself for causing them. Their feelings are their responsibility, not yours. You can be kind, but that kindness must begin with you, with self-love and boundaries. If their actions have led them to being alone, that is not your responsibility.

If you waver internally, do not share this with the gaslighter, who will use any opening to pry your doors wide. Find trustworthy confidants, such as a friend or therapist. Write your feelings in a journal. Meditate, reflect, or pray. Listen to your deepest instincts.

As you maintain your distance, gaining a sort of "sobriety" from the relationship, allow yourself to enjoy facets of life from which you may have held yourself back. Allow yourself to playfully explore your passions and enjoy your freedom!

You can expect resistance, intrusion, and pushback from the gaslighter. Be prepared, and know that it is no reflection on the rightness of your decision to end contact. Remain resolute. Be consistent. If necessary, consider a restraining order. Their attempts will likely lessen over time, but that is not an indication that you should let down your walls. Persist as the behavior decreases, and eventually, your barriers will stick.

The following exercises were designed to help you craft plans for your unique circumstances and needs.

EXERCISE 1: MAKING A PLAN

In this step of breaking free from gaslighting, we have explored various relationship scenarios and potential ways to reduce or end contact. The following decision tree can help you assess which response may be right for your unique scenario.

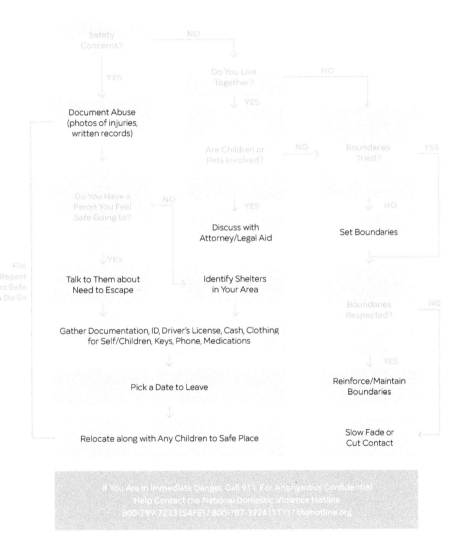

EXERCISE 2:

The answer to this question is probably yes. But if you're unsure, answer the following questions honestly to evaluate whether there is justification for letting down your guard. If all five questions are affirmative, it may be safe to let down some walls. But go slowly. There's no need to rush.

Y	N	Have they shown remorse?
Y	N	Have they admitted fault with specifics?
Y	N	Have they identified concrete, personal changes?
Y	N	Have they taken any action that demonstrates a changed heart (i.e., personal therapy, amends, sobriety)?
Y	N	Has a significant amount of time passed demonstrating changed patterns?

EXERCISE 3: SELF-CARE PLAN FOR AFTER THE BREAKUP

You've come to a conclusion; you've made your decision. Before setting your plan in motion, pause and consider what you'll need for personal after-action self-care. What will help you deal with any grief, loneliness, or misgivings? Consider supportive people, fulfilling activities, and things that soothe your emotions, and list them below.

_____

_____

_____

_____

_____

_____

_____

As you reduce or eliminate contact with the gaslighter in your life, you make space to look forward. You realize that you desire and deserve healthy relationships but may lack the confidence to create them. Don't fall into the trap of self-protective solitude if your heart yearns for more. In the final section, we will explore what defines a healthy relationship so that you are empowered to break the cycle of unhealthy connections for good.

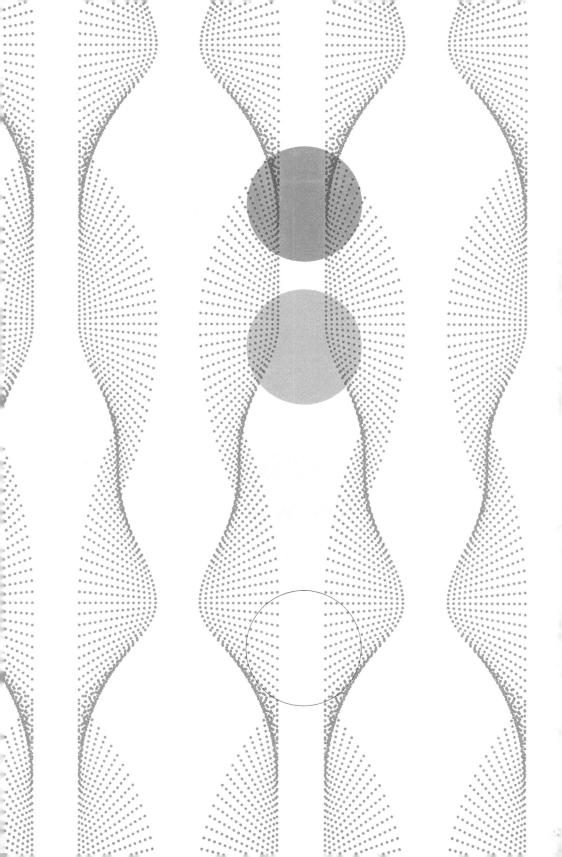

STEP 7:
DEVELOP HEALTHY RELATIONSHIPS AND BREAK THE CYCLE FOR GOOD

It is time to dream and hope. Time to look ahead and envision what you want to nurture in your life. Having determined what you do not want in your life, you have created space for what you do desire. In this chapter, we will discuss markers of healthy relationships and explore the possibilities for cultivating a new relational reality in your life.

MOVING FORWARD

Moving forward means grieving what was lost, maintaining boundaries set, and evaluating what you want in your life. Allow yourself to dream and to imagine. This is a very personal process. For some, moving forward may mean pursuing dreams long left dormant. You might return to school, seek a new job, explore a new hobby, or join an activity where you can meet others with whom to cultivate friendship—or perhaps something more.

For those newly single, know that remaining so can be a perfectly healthy, strong option. For those who desire a committed relationship, continue to work on your own inner healing, so that you aren't tempted to fill a felt hole with the first available relationship. Instead, you become ready to bring your whole self to another whole being.

BREAKING THE CYCLE

If you are hoping to kindle new relationships, whether romantic, platonic, collective/spiritual, or employment-based, you may be wary of falling into old traps—and rightly so. A study published in *Social Psychology Quarterly* found that people tend to gravitate toward relationships that confirm their preexisting beliefs about themselves, whether positive or negative. Our need to avoid cognitive dissonance—the mental discomfort that comes from holding conflicting beliefs—often overrules the pull toward the healthy relationships we truly desire. In other words, we tend to be more comfortable with what is familiar, even if that means abuse. It is imperative, therefore, to recognize the powerful pull toward familiarity if you wish to resist this gravity, create new, wholesome patterns in your life, and counter negative beliefs about yourself with radical self-love.

If you grew up with emotionally abusive relationships, experienced ongoing gaslighting from your family in adulthood, and perhaps fell into similarly patterned friendships or romantic relationships, emotionally abusive patterns may be all you really know. You must break the cycle in order to set yourself free. This requires honing your ability to spot a gaslighter, breaking codependency patterns, clarifying what you are seeking, and identifying signs of healthy people.

SPOTTING A GASLIGHTER

You want to avoid becoming entangled with a gaslighter again, knowing better than anyone how hard it can be to leave. Fortunately, by this point, you have familiarized yourself with gaslighting tactics and the cycles they follow. You have learned to listen to your inner voice and honor your intuition. As scary as it might feel to be on the verge of new beginnings, you are equipped to spot unknown gaslighters and sidestep toxic relationships before they begin.

Remember to be wary of those too quick to attach. There is no reason to rush. Give yourself days apart for reflection. Allow yourself the opportunity to journal or talk to a friend or therapist about what attracts you and what makes you uneasy.

Watch out for friends or dates who try to change you. You may not be perfect, but you deserve to be with someone who appreciates you for you—the messy, work-in-progress, beautiful mosaic that you are. In healthy relationships, unconditional acceptance comes first, which empowers and roots you in security to choose growth. Love is not something to be earned.

Distance yourself from controlling people. Those who take an authoritarian approach based on gender, age, race, or positional differences may ultimately use it to abuse you, even if they appear chivalrous now. You are less than no one, nor intrinsically greater. Demand and expect an egalitarian reciprocity of mutual respect.

Continue to review and apply the skills you have acquired throughout this book. Know that you owe your allegiance to no one. You can be kind and still say, "No, thank you" or "That doesn't work for me." Set your boundaries in advance and practice verbalizing them, know your exit strategies, and be courageous in communication. You are worthy of the self-care such boundaries represent. You deserve to say no to what is not right for you.

Dealing with Unsupportive People

You know your worth. You know what you do and don't want in your life. But not everyone will be supportive. Make peace with not pleasing everyone, whether in leaving a former relationship or starting a new one. Set clear boundaries, indicating that your decision is made and you do not wish to discuss it further. Give yourself permission to exit conversations where you are not respected.

In some circumstances, your decision to cut contact with a gaslighter may impact others whom you love, such as siblings of a parent you have decided not to see. You may wish, if you have the emotional space, to listen to their feelings. You can empathize while stopping short of defending yourself or negotiating boundaries you have carefully designed. This may even lead to a productive conversation about ways to connect without involving emotionally abusive dynamics.

Your job is to protect your own emotional and physical space. You do not need to make everyone else happy. You may care, while allowing them to work through their own feelings, just as you have learned to do for yourself.

PRACTICING SKILLS EVERY DAY

You've done much inner work as you've read through this book and completed each of the exercises. Continue to practice the skills, reinforce the boundaries, and work on the self-care plans you have developed throughout this process. Keep growing in your self-love, self-esteem, and self-confidence. As you continue this mindful inner work, you will find it becoming easier. Keep at it. You are worth it.

LOOKING FOR HEALTHY RELATIONSHIPS (WHEN YOU ARE READY)

Humans, like all mammals, are relational by nature. We are born dependent on others, flourish through secure attachments, and suffer when isolated or neglected. People need people. You have been hurt in a place of core need, a place of significant vulnerability. This can make the idea of interdependence frightening or even loathsome. It's okay to take a little time to yourself. Healing often comes in the silence. But don't be afraid to open your heart again.

This does not necessarily mean romantic relationships, although they can be very meaningful sources of joy and companionship. Pursuing and embracing your relational needs may also take the form of new friendships, roommates, mentors, mentees, and surrogate parents or grandparents. When you are ready, explore the possibilities found in volunteering, group classes, healthy spiritual communities, gyms or clubs, or neighborhood associations. Mindful use of social media can be a valuable tool to breaking isolation, when used as a stepping-stone rather than a replacement for meaningful contact.

Only you can determine when you are ready to move forward. Listen to your heart, and lean in with courage and the hard-won wisdom that now dwells inside you.

WHAT DOES A HEALTHY RELATIONSHIP LOOK LIKE?

Reviewing the data from the lab, David noticed a discrepancy. He cringed inwardly, knowing he had to bring this error to the attention of his boss. It was a matter of safety.

Maria was gracious when David approached. She thanked him for bringing the error to her attention. As he left her office, he heard her on the phone with management. Expecting the worst, he paused to listen and was surprised to hear her taking full responsibility for the research delay. The next day as the team gathered at the round table for the morning briefing, Maria made note of David's catch, praising his attention to detail while encouraging continued vigilance from the team.

Healthy relationships are distinguished by mutual respect and support and an egalitarian mindset. In healthy relationships, people consistently demonstrate kindness and compassion. Honesty is inherent to the relationship, creating emotional safety and trust.

Healthy relationships are not flawless. When mistakes are made or unkind words spewed, the offender demonstrates genuine remorse, takes responsibility, and shows a change in behavior. Forgiveness is extended without keeping score.

In a healthy relationship, you feel like your best self. You enjoy being with the other person and feel confident and comfortable. You don't fear judgment or embarrassment, because you know you are embraced for exactly who you are, just as you are.

When Dan met Sean, he kept waiting for the other shoe to drop. He was familiar with the pattern: swept off feet, professions of love, then sudden violence or rejection. When it didn't happen, he began to push for the inevitable. He told Sean every dirty secret about himself. Sean just looked at him tenderly and said, "The more I know you, the more deeply I love you."

As the years passed, Dan slowly came to trust that something was different with Sean. He wasn't like Dan's parents, who threw him out when he revealed his full self to them. He wasn't like any of his previous unreliable boyfriends. Sean listened intently when Dan spoke. He reminded Dan of his strengths. He held him when he cried, never shaming his pain. He respected Dan's physical boundaries. Sean made Dan feel safe.

Sometimes a person with a history of painful relationships stumbles into a healthy relationship without recognizing what a treasure they have found. Usually, the disconnect between expectations and experience causes that individual to retreat, lose interest, or sabotage a good thing. But sometimes they realize that they have struck emotional gold and hold fast.

What if there were a way to intentionally seek out healthy relationships, whether romantic or platonic, without waiting to fall into them serendipitously? What would that require?

To begin with, you need to know what you are looking for. This involves two things. First, you must have a clear concept of what healthy relationships look like. Second, it helps to have a vision of what your personal ideals might be. Supporting these two elements is a belief in your fundamental worthiness of respect or love.

With these two lists in mind, put yourself in situations where like-minded individuals might also be. If you meet someone with whom you feel a sense of connection, go slowly. Healthy relationships are not rushed. There is no need for hurry. Enjoy the dance of getting to know someone new, taking time to listen to your instincts along the way.

EQUITABLE RELATIONSHIPS

Equality is perhaps the clearest marker of a healthy relationship. In an equitable relationship, both parties share power and give equal deference to each other. There is no assumed hierarchy based upon gender or gender identity, race, age, income, immigration history, family background, education, sexual orientation, or any other characteristic or trait. Your own history is left in the past and not held against you to establish dominance through guilt trips or shame.

Roles and division of labor are negotiated, rather than assumed, and based upon interests and skills, or work may be shared equally. Each member of the couple or group is given equal voice, and that voice is heard, respected, and considered in decision-making.

Care is also reciprocal. You are not expected to be the emotional support pet for the other, and you are not given the constant role of cheerleader or expected to always wear a happy face. Both partners know they are safe and welcome to share their full range of emotional experiences in a direct and honest way with each other, anticipating care, compassion, and support in response.

STORIES OF EQUITABLE RELATIONSHIPS

Equality in relationships shows up in many ways. Consider the following contrasts.

Growing up, Darnell watched his mother do all the cooking, cleaning, and tending to the children before and after her job. It was always Mom who showed up for school meetings and took them to appointments. His father went to his office job, watched sports on TV as dinner was prepared, and punished the children when rules were broken

When Darnell got married, he and Janae tried a new approach. They enjoyed cooking meals together, getting the kids involved, and took turns washing the dishes afterward while the other helped the children get ready for bed. Each parent tucked in one child, then they relaxed together, catching up on TV shows they both enjoyed. When a child misbehaved, the parent present at the time spoke with that child directly, hearing their side, guiding them toward better choices, and teaching them to make amends.

• • •

Katarina was feeling tentative about new relationships. She was reeling from the loss of her friendship with Lucia. Katarina had called out Lucia for gossiping about her, and Lucia then gaslit Katarina and blocked her abruptly on social media.

When Katarina chatted with Mai while volunteering together at the animal shelter, they always found themselves laughing. One day Mai suggested they meet for coffee, soliciting Katarina's input on where to go and what day might work well. She seemed genuinely interested in her thoughts, even when they disagreed. As the friendship progressed, both friends kept each other's confidences, and each respected when the other needed time or space. Katarina came to feel secure that their friendship was strong enough for her to show up as her true, full self.

CARING FOR YOURSELF EVERY DAY

As you have worked through this book, you've learned to recognize the signs and cycles of gaslighting and hopefully grown to accept the truth of what has been happening in your life. You've wrestled with the anger and grief over these implications. You have examined your existing boundaries and developed new ones to fortify the life you wish to lead. And you've begun to dream and imagine what healthy relationships might look like for you.

Most important, I hope you have internalized greater self-love. No matter what you decide about your present circumstances, continue to make yourself a priority. Practice self-care and grow in self-confidence. Make time for healthy relationships and the things that fill your heart. You deserve peace, and you deserve love. Let that love flow gently from within and water the soil of your life.

These final exercises are designed to facilitate, guide, and strengthen your right and resolve to live a fulfilling, gaslighting-free life.

EXERCISE 1: EVALUATING CURRENT RELATIONSHIPS

Consider your current relationships. For each category, identify one significant relationship. If a category does not apply to you, simply skip it, or write in a more applicable relationship from another category. What are some positive or negative indicators of health in each? What things could you do to improve that relationship and your enjoyment of it?

	Unhealthy	Healthy	Ways to Improve
Friendship			
Romantic Partner			
Parents			
Sibling			
Workplace			
Other			

EXERCISE 2: DEFINING YOUR IDEAL

Describe your ideal friendship, mentorship, romantic relationship, or workplace environment. Focus on the type of relationship you have just exited or reduced. Try to define your ideal in terms of what you want it to be like, rather than what you don't want to see. For example, "I want to date someone adventurous" is more visionary than "I don't want to be with someone who just watches TV every night."

EXERCISE 3: DRAWING IT TOGETHER

For this final exercise, take your journal and spend some time in reflection. Read back over all the exercises you have completed and the writing prompts to which you have responded. Reflect on what you have learned, how you have grown, and what has changed. Make a final entry, exploring these questions:

- What have you learned about yourself?
- How have you changed?
- What has changed in your life?
- What commitments are you willing to make going forward to reinforce this growth and make self-love and self-care a constant?

Remember: you are worthy.

A FINAL WORD

As a therapist, I'm often asked, "How could they do this to me?" Please know that it isn't your job to make sense of wrongs committed against you. All you need to know is that you never deserved this and that you deserve love. You always have; you always will. The gaslighting and the cruelty it concealed weren't really about you. They were about them, their insecurity, their narcissism, and their sadism.

Let go of trying to change gaslighters, and honor yourself and your needs. Remember your inherent worth and continue to grow in self-love. You deserve to engage in self-care every day, no matter how busy you are or what kind of day you have had. Be mindful of the negative messages that try to sneak back in, reminding yourself of their origins in the abuse and dismissing them firmly, with compassion.

Keep in mind that not every relationship bump or misunderstanding indicates a gaslighter or a need to withdraw. Allow yourself discretion to work through messy problems, which crop up in every healthy relationship, while knowing and holding your boundaries with others. Continue to listen to your intuition, giving yourself permission to feel your feelings. Talk to trusted friends who will be honest with you, and journal your experiences to help sort through and analyze baffling communication.

If parts of this book resonated with you and other parts didn't connect, that's okay. Take what is useful to you and leave the rest. Gaslighting relationships are diverse and have varying levels of impact, depending upon the type, timing, and duration of the relationship. Consequently, your experiences and recovery process may vary. You are unique, and your journey is your own.

Know that you are worthy of love and respect. Any experience or message that told you otherwise was a lie. Hold on tightly to this truth. Let it guide you forward as you seek out and build the life you desire.

RESOURCES

SUGGESTED READING FOR CONTINUED GROWTH

Black, Claudia. *Repeat after Me: A Workbook for Adult Children Overcoming Dysfunctional Family Systems.* Rev. ed. Las Vegas, NV: Central Recovery Press, 2018.

A guide to overcoming dysfunctional family systems and breaking free of codependency.

Brown, Brené. *Men, Women, and Worthiness: The Experience of Shame and the Power of Being Enough.* Louisville, CO: Sounds True, 2012.

An exploration of the power of shame and a guide to cultivating a sense of worthiness in who you are.

Maté, Gabor. *When the Body Says No: Exploring the Stress-Disease Connection.* Hoboken, NJ: John Wiley & Sons, 2011.

An exploration of the connection between stress and disease.

Moreland, Mike. *EFT Tapping: Quick and Simple Exercises to De-stress, Re-energize and Overcome Emotional Problems Using Emotional Freedom Technique.* Scotts Valley, CA: CreateSpace, 2014.

A guide to using tapping techniques to decrease and manage emotional overwhelm.

Shapiro, Francine. *Getting Past Your Past: Take Control of Your Life with Self-Help Techniques from EMDR Therapy.* New York: Rodale, 2012.

An introduction to EMDR therapy with adapted techniques you can use at home to gain greater emotional freedom.

Tawwab, Nedra Glover. *Set Boundaries, Find Peace: A Guide to Reclaiming Yourself.* New York: TarcherPerigee, 2021.
An introduction to boundaries and how to set them.

Van der Kolk, Bessel A. *The Body Keeps the Score: Brain, Mind, and Body in the Healing of Trauma.* New York: Penguin Books, 2015.
An exploration of how unprocessed trauma reveals itself through the body and the urgency of addressing trauma for holistic health.

INTERNET RESOURCES AND CRISIS HOTLINES FOR SUPPORT

American Psychological Association Psychologist Locator
Locator.APA.org
To find a licensed psychologist in your area.

American Association for Marriage and Family Therapy Therapist Locator
AAMFT.org/Directories/Find_a_Therapist.aspx
To find a licensed marriage and family therapist in your area.

Psychology Today: Find a Therapist
PsychologyToday.com/us/therapists
To find a licensed therapist (psychologist, marriage and family therapist, clinical social worker, licensed professional counselor) in your area.

Brainspotting Directory
Brainspotting.com/directory
To learn more about Brainspotting and find a therapist certified in this approach.

Eye Movement Desensitization and Reprocessing International Association: Find a Therapist Directory
EMDRIA.org/find-a-therapist

To learn more about eye movement desensitization and reprocessing (EMDR) therapy and find a therapist certified in this approach.

Rape, Abuse & Incest National Network (RAINN)
RAINN.org
Resources, hotline, and information from RAINN.

National Suicide Prevention Lifeline
SuicidePreventionLifeline.org
Resources and hotline for suicide prevention.

National Domestic Violence Hotline
TheHotline.org
Resources and hotline for those caught in the cycle of domestic violence.

National Suicide Prevention Lifeline:
800-273-8255 *United States*
9-8-8 *coming July 2022* *United States*
833-456-4566 or text 45645 *Canada*

National Human Trafficking Hotline:
888-373-7888 *United States*
833-900-1010 *Canada*

National Sexual Assault Hotline:
800-656-4673 *United States*

National Domestic Violence Hotline:
800-799-7233 United States TTY: 800-787-3224 *United States*

Canadian Resource Centre for Victims of Crime:
877-232-2610 or text 613-208-0747 Canada

All other emergencies:
9-1-1 *United States and Canada*

REFERENCES

American Psychiatric Association. *Diagnostic and Statistical Manual of Mental Disorders.* 5th ed. Arlington, VA: American Psychiatric Association, 2013.

Carney, Michelle Mohr, and John R. Barner. "Prevalence of Partner Abuse: Rates of Emotional Abuse and Control." *Partner Abuse* 3, no. 3 (2012): 286–335. doi.org/10.1891/1946 -6560.3.3.286.

Eastwick, Paul W., Eli J. Finkel, Tamar Krishnamurti, and George Loewenstein. "Mispredicting Distress Following Romantic Breakup: Revealing the Time Course of the Affective Forecasting Error." *Journal of Experimental Social Psychology* 44, no. 3 (May 2008): 800–807. doi.org/10.1016/j.jesp.2007.07.001.

Felitti, Vincent J., Robert F. Anda, Dale Nordenberg, David F. Williamson, Alison M. Spitz, Valerie Edwards, Mary P. Koss, and James S. Marks. "Relationship of Childhood Abuse and Household Dysfunction to Many of the Leading Causes of Death in Adults: The Adverse Childhood Experiences (ACE) Study." *American Journal of Preventive Medicine* 14, no. 4 (1998): 245–58. doi.org/10.1016/S0749-3797(98)00017-8.

Grand, David. *Brainspotting: The Revolutionary New Therapy for Rapid and Effective Change.* Boulder, CO: Sounds True, 2013.

Harris, Russ. *The Complete Set of Client Handouts and Worksheets from ACT Books.* 2014. TheHappinessTrap.com /upimages/Complete_Worksheets_2014.pdf.

Kidd, Ian James, José Medina, and Gaile Pohlhaus, Jr., eds. *The Routledge Handbook of Epistemic Injustice.* Routledge Handbooks in Philosophy. London and New York: Routledge, 2017.

Riggs, Damien W., and Clare Bartholomaeus. "Gaslighting in the Context of Clinical Interactions with Parents of Transgender Children." *Sexual and Relationship Therapy* 33, no 4 (2018): 382–94. doi.org/10.1080/14681994.2018.1444274.

Robinson, Dawn T., and Lynn Smith-Lovin. "Selective Interaction as a Strategy for Identity Maintenance: An Affect Control Model." *Social Psychology Quarterly* 55, no. 1 (March 1992): 12–28. jstor.org/stable/2786683.

Siegel, Daniel J. *The Developing Mind: Toward a Neurobiology of Interpersonal Experience.* New York: Guilford Press, 1999.

———. *Mindsight: The New Science of Personal Transformation.* New York: Bantam, 2010.

Sweet, Paige L. "The Sociology of Gaslighting." *American Sociological Review* 84, no. 5 (October 2019): 851–75. doi.org /10.1177/0003122419874843.

Walker, Pete. *The Tao of Fully Feeling: Harvesting Forgiveness out of Blame.* Lafayette, CA: Azure Coyote, 1995.

INDEX

National Suicide
Prevention
Lifeline, 30
Needs, 89–90, 106
Neuroplasticity, 34, 88

O

Obligation, feelings
of, 69
Oxytocin, 58

P

Peaceful place
exercise, 96
Personality
disorders, 8–9
Physical abuse, 31
Power dynamics,
10–11
Preferences, 89–90
Pushback, dealing
with, 126–127

R

Relationship patterns
enablers, 61–62
ghosting/
stonewalling,
60–61
hoovering, 58–60
identifying, 67
love-bombing-
devaluing-
discarding, 55–58
Relationships, healthy
developing, 36
equality in, 141–143
exercises, 144–146
looking for, 139

principles of, 24,
63, 139–141
Responsibility, refusal
to take, 20–21

S

Sadistic gaslighters,
11–12
Self-awareness, 108
Self-care, 90–91,
98, 133
Self-compassion,
85–86
Self-confidence,
92–93
Self-esteem, 92
Self-focus, 36
Self-love, 90
Self-talk, negative,
86, 97
Siegel, Daniel, 7, 94
Slow fade approach
to leaving,
125–126
Splitting, 21–22
Stockholm
syndrome, 75
Stonewalling, 60–61
Suicidal thoughts,
30, 74–75
Support networks,
84, 128
Sweet, Paige, 10

T

Therapy, 86–88
Trauma, 33–34
Triangulation, 22
Trust, 93–94

U

Undermining
accomplishments,
17–18

V

Van der Kolk,
Bessel, 94

Y

Yoga, 94

ACKNOWLEDGMENTS

Writing this book was both a dream and a challenge. It would not have been possible without the endless support and encouragement of my dear partner and husband, Shane, who always believes in me, cheers me on, and picks up the slack (even more than usual!) when my time becomes harried. Thank you for your sacrifices to help make this dream a reality and for reading all my raw material late at night.

Luke, my sweet son, thank you for always noticing when I need a chocolate perk or a hug, for your encouragement, and for your insightful reflections as I discussed challenges in the writing process, far surpassing the wisdom of your age. And you're right, our cat Ringo does deserve a shout-out for sitting at my feet every night while I wrote!

Robin Dykema, my supportive big sister, thank you for beta reading my sample material and helping me refine it to catch the attention of the publisher, and for believing in me.

Mayra Gonzalez, my dear friend, thank you for lending your social work perspective to this material and for cheering me on. Nancy James, thank you for sharing your expert review and input to key clinical sections, and for your cherished friendship and encouragement. Lynn Sanders, thank you for the spiral staircase analogy and for so much more. Natalie Aalders-Price, my longest friend, I love you for believing in my writing dreams since childhood and helping me ground my sanity when I questioned my own truths. To my friends and family who provided encouragement, check-ins, coffee, subversive gifts, and celebration—thank you. You all make life beautiful.

Jesse Aylen and Mariah Gumpert, my editors, thank you for the thoughtful suggestions, edits, and words of affirmation along the way, and to the entire team at Callisto for shaping this project and carrying it into the world.

Thank you to everyone who shared with me your stories of being gaslit. May this book be an encouragement to you.

ABOUT THE AUTHOR

Deborah Vinall, PsyD, LMFT, is a licensed marriage and family therapist and doctor of psychology, certified in both EMDR and Brainspotting therapy. She incorporates these approaches into her work with survivors of trauma and difficult relationships in her private practice. Deborah has spoken as a subject matter expert on human trafficking and domestic violence at colleges and nonprofits across Southern California. She was awarded the EMDR Research Foundation's Sandra Wilson Memorial Dissertation Grant Award for her research on the impacts on and treatment response of survivors of mass shootings. Born and raised in Kelowna, Canada, Deborah presently lives in Southern California with her husband and son.